CHABAD OF XXXXXXXX
973-895 3070
BEKHOR / TILSON

ArtScroll Series®

Rabbi Nosson Scherman / Rabbi Meir Zlotowitz

General Editors

Published by

Mesorah Publications, ltd

ARYEH B.
TABACK

True stories of

everyday

miracles

THE DIRECTOR

FIRST EDITION
First Impression ... April 2003

Published and Distributed by
MESORAH PUBLICATIONS, LTD.
4401 Second Avenue / Brooklyn, N.Y 11232

Distributed in Europe by
LEHMANNS
Unit E, Viking Industrial Park
Rolling Mill Road
Jarrow, Tyne & Wear, NE32 3DP
England

Distributed in Israel by
SIFRIATI / A. GITLER
6 Hayarkon Street
Bnei Brak 51127

Distributed in Australia and New Zealand by
GOLDS WORLD OF JUDAICA
3-13 William Street
Balaclava, Melbourne 3183
Victoria Australia

Distributed in South Africa by
KOLLEL BOOKSHOP
Shop 8A Norwood Hypermarket
Norwood 2196, Johannesburg, South Africa

ARTSCROLL SERIES®
THE DIRECTOR
© *Copyright 2003, by* MESORAH PUBLICATIONS, Ltd.
4401 Second Avenue / Brooklyn, N.Y. 11232 / (718) 921-9000 / www.artscroll.com

ISBN:
1-57819-734-1 (hard cover)
1-57819-735-X (paperback)

Typography by CompuScribe at ArtScroll Studios, Ltd.

Printed in the United States of America by Noble Book Press Corp.
Bound by Sefercraft, Quality Bookbinders, Ltd., Brooklyn N.Y. 11232

This book is lovingly dedicated in memory of
my mother and teacher

חיה אסתר ע״ה
בת יבלחט״א
זאב יהושע נ״י

Adele Taback ע״ה

Raised in a home steeped in Jewish values and tradition,
Her burning desire for the truth
Led her to a life filled with Torah and Mitzvos,
Filled with life.

She was able to give so much life to others
As a loving mother,
As a midwife and childbirth insructor,
And as an inspiring role model to the women of Johannesburg.

She left this world for the next
    with her two pure daughters at her side,
Not for a lack of life
But rather at its zenith,
A living example of what life is really about.

ת.נ.צ.ב.ה.

ope and trepidation are two very diverse emotions, yet both simultaneously fill my heart as I ready this work for publication. The hope is a deep-seated one, a fervent desire that these pages in some way succeed in transmitting to you, the reader, the feelings and inspiration which I have experienced while preparing them. The person I am now is vastly different from the person I was when I started the process, and the world is a different place through the new eyes I have found. Trepidation, too, grips my heart, for to tell a story is to be entrusted with one of the most precious commodities, a commodity ever so fragile, a commodity called "the truth." It is a characteristic of the Divine, something that finite beings can only approach through much toil and effort, and one which I have fought to preserve throughout the creative stages of this work. Nevertheless, I ask the forbearance of the many people who told me their stories, the people who entrusted me with their very lives, for I am certain that elements of the stories they lived through may seem unrelated to the words which I have used to describe them. Notwithstanding this, I have done everything in my power to bring to you, the reader, the details and facts of each and every remarkable story in as real and honest a manner as possible. With the exception of one or two stories, every account in this collection was heard firsthand from the people who experienced them. Great effort was expended in following up on the smallest of details, to ensure that every facet of every story is accurate. Nevertheless, I have taken the liberty of changing certain minor and inconsequential details such as names and places in some of the stories to protect the identities of the people concerned.

I would like to acknowledge the roles the following people have played, both directly and indirectly, in helping me to reach this stage.

I would like to acknowledge the roles the following people have played, both directly and indirectly, in helping me to reach this stage:

Rabbi Menachem Raff, who first suggested I write this book, has a major share not only in the work before you but also in its author. He is a consummate builder of people, and I thank him for having enough faith in me to give me faith in myself. His predecessor Rav Aharon Pfeuffer zt"l also shaped me tremendously. Although I was only bar mitzvah at the time of his passing, the passion and honesty with which he lived his life seared an indelible impression onto my neshamah. Heartfelt gratitude goes to R' David Emanuel, whose support has given my family and me the strength and courage to weather the storms of life, and whose joy has been with us at every *simchah*. Robert and Perel have been pillars of stability and encouragement for my family and me, especially when our entire world trembled beneath us, and I am exceptionally grateful to them.

The characters in this book are all real, and I am indebted to each and every one for sharing with me their stories. Kudos are also due to Joan Wainer for her advice on the manuscript, and to Devora Rhein for her masterful editing of the final text. A special thanks goes to Ernest Mozansky and David Reuben for their advice regarding some of the more technical aspects of writing a book. I am grateful also to David Sacks, who generously allowed me to utilize his scholarly research on the South African Jewish community as the basis of my introduction on that subject.

I thank all of the various people I have had the opportunity of teaching here in Johannesburg, for although you were the students, it is I that has learned the most.

Kevin, friends like you hardly exist in today's world, and I am who I am today thanks to your friendship and support. Thanks boet.

Granny and Grampa, you are pillars of strength, and your positivity and optimism have allowed us to face the greatest challenges together. Heather, your courage and care have done so much for us, and I thank you from the bottom of my heart for helping to captain our "big ship." Abba, your strength, counsel, and the example you have set for us have had a profound impact on my life, and I am eternally indebted to you for everything that you have done for me. Dani, Orit, Ora, Yehuda, Adina, and Sara — you guys mean the world to me. Imma, your example will remain with me for as long as I live.

Tamar, thanks for having me.

And last but not least, my humble but heartfelt thanks go to The Director...

▪ Introduction

t is the type of script that stage directors dream about. A drama so unique, so unusual, that it will only run one time. A single showing, during which each of the thousands of actors will cross the stage but once, during which time they must act as if their entire world depends on this performance. There are no rehearsals, no second chances. This show is in real time. The actors in the cast have given this strange production a name of their own, a title of endearment. They call it — life.

What makes this production so unique, so different from any other, is the fact that its roles are intertwined as if part of a complex tapestry. It is a play in which every character has an opportunity to be the hero, the star, or, conversely, the villain. Every actor who emerges onto the stage from the wings has a chance to play the lead role, every actor has the potential to receive a standing ovation when he or she returns to the real world backstage, behind those heavy curtains.

But we must realize a fascinating yet little-recognized truth. Observe for a moment that not only is *he* the protagonist, not only is *she* playing the lead role of this surreal production, but at the same time, they are mere "extras," the backdrop in yet another character's act, playing secondary roles in someone else's production. Every actor is simultaneously occupying center stage, face glowing under the spotlight, while at the same time but a prop in someone else's solo. This should fill our hearts with awe and fear of He Who choreographs this infinitely complex drama we call Life, He Who ensures this seamless fusion of foreground and backdrop into one perfect reality.

For the most part, the Director has chosen to remain unseen, concealing Himself from the view of His subjects. Never will a single actor see Him directly. Notwithstanding this, an experienced eye, an eye that seeks Him with unswerving honesty, will see His handiwork and imprint at every turn. Open your eyes, small speck in this immense world, and you will see Him directing your every step.

This collection of stories represents infinitesimally short episodes in this monumental drama, through which simple and unassuming people glimpsed the awesome power coordinating their lives. Let us absorb these stories, so that we too might learn to see this Power. Then, let us pay homage to the Director.

▪ A Brief Note on South Africa and its Jewish Community

The Republic of South Africa forms the lower jaw of the skull-shaped African continent. It is a vast country, covering over one million square kilometers – twice the size of France – and is surrounded by nearly three thousand kilometers of pristine coastline. To the east and south, the warm Indian Ocean forms her boundary, while to the west the icy South Atlantic laps her shores. Only to the north is South Africa bounded by neighbors: Namibia, Botswana, Zimbabwe, Mozambique, and Swaziland. It is a richly diverse land; from the towering Drakansberg mountain range in the east, laced with icy alpine streams; to the dry and arid northwest, and the deserts of Kalahari and Karoo. In the northeast, the massive Kruger National Park, alone larger than the entire State of Israel, forms one of the most expansive wildlife refuges in the world. South Africa is a beautiful country, blessed with a mild and delightful climate, and a relaxed, easygoing way of life.

The South African Jewish community is well organized, with a deep attachment to Jewish traditional values. The community goes back a long way, with persons of Jewish descent having found their way to the Cape from the earliest beginnings of white settlement. Records of Jewish settlers date as far back as the 18th century.

The main influx, however, began many years later. The discovery of diamonds and gold between 1867 and 1886, which was the beginning of South Africa's industrial development, attracted large numbers of immigrants from many parts of the world, among them many Jews. Some of these Jews were among the founders and developers of South Africa's rich diamond- and gold-mining industries. Their achievements gave them status and influence beyond their numbers. They were friends and confidants of national figures and some became civic leaders.

Of course, most of the Jews who came to South Africa, like most others who arrived, did not become mining magnates. In fact, a majority of the Jewish immigrants were fleeing religious oppression in Czarist Russia and were very poor. For many, the streets were not paved with gold but with poverty. The early immigrants were mainly artisans and small traders. From 1882 to 1912 some 40,000 Jews entered the country. In the next forty years another 25,000 arrived, mainly from Lithuania, Latvia, and England; 8, 000 of them came as refugees from Nazi Germany in the 1930's. After World War II, there began to be moderate influxes of Jews from Israel and Zimbabwe. Most South African Jews today were born in South Africa.

The census on October 10, 1996 showed the total South African population at just under 40 million. Today there are an estimated 85,000 Jews, compared to 120,000 in 1980. The majority live in the Johannesburg area, the other large metropolitan concentration being in Cape Town, with smaller communities in Durban and Pretoria. The cities of Port Elizabeth, East London, and Bloemfontein were once thriving Jewish centers, but have declined to a few hundred souls each, most of them elderly. Immigration has taken its toll on the Jewish population, with many qualified people seeking to escape the high-crime levels experienced in the country, especially in Johannesburg. Nevertheless, despite the specter of crime, there are many Jewish South Africans who remain committed to South Africa and the lifestyle they are able to lead there.

The Johannesburg Jewish community remains strong and cohesive, helped in the last twenty years by the fact that Jewish families have moved away from the city center, in favor of the more bucolic northern suburbs such as Sydenham, Dunkeld, Wendywood, Gallo Manor, and Glenhazel. Religious organizations are on par with those of any other country, with an effective *Chevrah Kaddisha*, *Beis Din*, and *Hatzalah* service in operation. The majority of Jewish children are still enrolled in Jewish day schools.

The South African Jewish community remains one of the Diaspora's crown jewels, and with Hashem's help will continue to thrive and grow until the coming of Mashiach, speedily in our days.

1

Act One: Momentous Moments

or twenty-two years, a father mourns his missing son, over two decades of anguish, haunted by memories of the closeness between them. The boy was only 17 when he left his father. The only remains the poor grieving man got back was the child's bloodstained coat. Convinced that his son had been torn apart by wild animals, he grieved inconsolably, certain that he would descend into his own grave still mourning the death of his favorite child. An entire family is plunged into grief, for their lost boy and for his inconsolable father.

After twenty-two years, the child is discovered alive, a grown man and a ruler in a faraway land. The news is gently relayed to his broken father. Unable to believe what he is being told, it takes much convincing before he finally believes what has happened. His heart bursting with emotion, he prepares to undertake the arduous journey to meet his long-lost son.

The reunion day finally arrives.

Hot tears course down Yosef's face as he clings fiercely to his beloved father. But wait! What is this? Yaakov Avinu cries not. What is happening? Where are all the pent-up tears of the last twenty-two years? What is Yaakov preoccupied with?

He seems to be murmuring something.

What is he saying?

Listen closely, for he is reciting the Shema.

What an unusual thing to be doing at such an emotionally charged moment. Why should Yaakov suddenly remember the *Shema*?

There is deep meaning behind his act. It was the time for Shema, because Yaakov chose to use the moment of inspiration to come closer to his Maker. Hundreds of emotions crowded our patriarch's head, but flying proud above all of them was a feeling of tremendous closeness to the Almighty, an emotion he chose to capture for eternity at that instant. And he said to himself, "Shema Yisrael Hashem Elokeinu Hashem echad!"

It is imperative that we open our eyes to the Hand of the Director which coordinates our lives, and that we capture the inspiration that comes from the major events we experience. Every being will experience these moments at least once in a lifetime, but all too often will fail to capitalize on them.

▪ Roots and Branches

There are numerous blessings that a Jew makes over unusual phenomena and experiences. One of these is a special blessing one recites on visiting a place where one was saved from imminent danger by means of a miracle. The blessing is recited by the person concerned to thank Hashem for having performed the miracle on his behalf. Interestingly there is another blessing recited over a miracle, designated not for the person to whom it occurred, but for a person to make when encountering a place where a miracle was performed for his father, mother, or forebearer as a result of which their lives were spared.

We tend to forget that our destinies are shaped not only by the events which occur during our own lifetimes but also by those things which occurred to our parents, grandparents, and all of our ancestors prior to our arrival on this world. What follows is a personal anecdote which brought this message home to me.

Selig Saffer and Sarah Koppel were born in the town of Kelm in Lithuania during the 1860's. After their marriage sometime during the late 19th century, Selig set up a small shoe-making business, in order to support his wife, and later his growing family. By the turn of the century, however, the deflated economic conditions in Eastern Europe were prompting many Jews to seek greener pastures, and at some stage during this time period, Selig and Sarah decided to follow suit. By that time, the Saffer family numbered fifteen individuals, including Selig, Sarah, their five sons, and their eight daughters, and it was decided that they would not all leave Kelm at the same time.

One of the destinations of choice among Jews of Lithuania in those years was Africa. After much deliberation, the Saffers decided to head for the Republic of South Africa, which was rumored to be a pleasant and prosperous place to settle. The last shots of the Boer War had reportedly been fired, and with the formation of the Rand Gold Mines, opportunities were apparently waiting to be grabbed. Thus, in 1903, Selig and Sarah's oldest daughter Leah, together with her husband Joseph, set sail for Cape Town aboard the Goyle Castle, which berthed in the Cape Town harbor on December 16, 1903. After a short period during which Joseph worked in Cape Town, the young couple eventually moved up to the burgeoning Johannesburg region. The first root of the Saffer family had now burrowed deep into the fertile South African soil.

In 1908, Max Saffer joined his sister in Johannesburg, and two years later on December 30, 1910, their brother Philip docked in Cape Town aboard the Gaika Castle. Over the next few years, more members of the family began arriving intermittently, until the First World War broke out, stranding Selig and Sarah together with their remaining children in Europe. It was not until July 1921 that they succeeded in getting to South Africa aboard the Britain. Finally the family was complete, or would have been if not for a terrible tragedy which had occurred a few years earlier.

The date was September 16, 1913, and at the time only three of the thirteen siblings had made it to South Africa. Of the three, only Leah was married, while her brothers Max and Philip remained single and worked with Leah's husband in what he called a "bottle-and-bag" venture. On that day, Philip and his older brother Max were tinkering with a broken gas stove. As they became more and more engrossed in the task, the telephone rang in another part of the house. The brothers debated with one another as to who would go to answer, and eventually Phillip grudgingly pried himself away and left the room. Moments later, a blast rocked the room he had just left. Something had gone wrong with the stove being repaired. Tragically, Max did not survive the blast. Philip was saved by the phone call.

Philip Saffer was my great-grandfather.

The extended Saffer family remains a close-knit unit to this very day. They have set up a support network and family fund with over four hundred members, some of whom are sixth-generation descendants of Selig and Sarah. Members meet regularly and are in constant contact with one another, sharing good news and bad and just being there for one another. The core of the family still remains in South Africa although there are members residing in all corners of the globe.

Many years ago, a beautiful family tree was drawn, graphically portraying the offshoots of the thirteen Saffer children. The artist, in a particularly poignant manner, depicted one of the branches as having been sawn off very close to the trunk. On the stump of the branch appears the name "Max."

The adjacent branch is long and healthy, with many shoots and sub-branches stemming from it. On this branch is penned the name "Philip." Toward the very tip of this branch, my name appears. I often look at the two branches, and wonder to myself: What would have been—? What would have been if not for that phone call—?

▪ Lifesaving Procedure

There is a well-known story told concerning the famous
Torah giant, Harav Aharon Kotler, z"tl, who fled Europe as it

*went up in flames in the mid-1900s. Rav Kotler was torn by
the decision regarding where to flee: On the one hand, the
prospect of settling in the Holy Land was very tempting, but it
was mitigated by the tremendous need for Torah leadership in
the United States. Rav Aharon had received a letter from the
great Rav Moshe Feinstein, zt"l, who had settled in America,
inviting him to help teach the Torah-thirsty community.*

*Unable to make a decision, Rav Kotler reportedly turned to an
age-old method of resolving such predicaments, known as the*
Goral HaGra. *This involves taking a* Chumash *or* Tanach *and
opening it in a specific manner to a random page. The person
performing the* goral *then reads the first verse he sees there.
This verse should offer him the advice that he needs.*

Rav Aharon reportedly opened a Chumash *randomly to
the verse ,"And Hashem said to Aharon, go to meet Moshe
in the desert…" (Shemos 4:27). Without much further
deliberation, Rav Aharon Kotler went to join Rav Moshe
Feinstein in the spiritual desert of America, where he led the
masses until his passing.*

*The following story is a modern-day echo of the one
above, and interestingly enough, it revolves around the
verses in the Torah immediately preceding the above-quoted
one. It occurred not long ago in the shul where I daven:*

Friday afternoons have their own special character in Jewish
homes. As the day marches steadily toward sunset, the chaos
and bedlam escalate until it seems as though the entire house is on
the verge of exploding. Kids shout, chickens cook, baths run,
brooms sweep; to an outsider it must seem as if the household is
rushing helter-skelter toward a rendezvous with disaster. And then
suddenly, everything becomes calm. A giant stop is placed in front
of all the week's activities and the home heaves a deep sigh of contentment in anticipation of the twenty-five hours of tranquility that
lie ahead.

It had been yet another long week for Steven Davies, a surgeon operating in the hospitals of Johannesburg. He was looking forward to the revitalizing rest of Shabbos. It had not been a completely ordinary week, however, because on Monday morning he had performed a *bris milah*, a circumcision. Steven had done the procedure only a few times in his life, and had consented to do it this time as a rare favor for a close friend. The experience had carried him through his busy week, but now it was time to relax and enjoy the Shabbos.

As his wife prepared the Shabbos candles, Steven rounded up his 13-year-old daughter and 6-year-old son and hurried them out to the car. They were to attend Friday-night *davening* at a nearby shul where he would leave his car parked for the duration of the day of rest. He bade his wife "Good Shabbos" and joined the children in the car. Shifting the car to reverse, Steven slowly began backing out of the driveway. As he passed through the gate at the end of the driveway, Steven suddenly went pale. Two men stood in the road with guns trained on him. His stomach lurched into his throat. They wanted his car.

As calmly as possible, Steven ordered the kids out of the car, and then slowly opened his own door. The assailants instructed them all to lie down on the ground and then, with guns aimed at their heads, they began frisking them for weapons or valuables. Steven held his breath and prayed that they would not harm him or the children. After what seemed like an eternity, the men jumped into the car, backed away, and roared off.

The car was found a short time later, abandoned on a side road after an antihijacking mechanism immobilized the vehicle.

Steven did not make it to shul that night, but on Shabbos morning, he headed toward the Yeshivah Maharsha Beis Midrash. He had extra motivation to go to shul that morning, for now he needed to recite *Bircas Hagomel*, the blessing one says to thank Hashem for saving one's life.

Steven was called up to the Torah for the sixth *aliyah* of the week's portion, *Shemos*. As he made his way up to the *bimah*, he made a mental note to listen carefully to what the portion was about. On previous occasions, Steven had noticed remarkable associations between the events in his life and the Torah portions for which he had been called up. He followed in the Torah carefully, and as the reader neared the end of the portion, a shiver ran up Steven's spine. The Torah described Moshe *Rabbeinu's* journey from the land of Midyan, where he had been in hiding, to the land of Egypt where his people were enslaved. At his side was his wife Tzipporah and their two sons, one of whom had been born recently and was yet to be circumcised.

As they traveled, the Torah relates how Hashem intercepted Moshe and wanted to take his life. Tzipporah realized that her husband's life was at risk as a result of his not having circumcised his son, and she quickly grabbed an instrument and performed the *milah*. Moshe's life was saved as a result of her prompt reaction. On seeing what she had done, Tzipporah declared the following words, words which echoed through Steven's head for days after that unforgettable Shabbos: "*Chasan damim lamulos,*" which is translated by the *Targum Yerushalmi* to mean, "How dear is the blood of circumcision, which saved a husband from the hands of the Angel of Death."

After the reader had completed the portion, Steven recited the blessing over the Torah followed by the blessing of *Hagomel*: "Blessed are You, Hashem, King of the universe, Who bestows good things upon the guilty, Who has bestowed every goodness upon me."

The congregation replied fervently: "Amen. May He Who bestowed goodness upon you continue to bestow every goodness upon you forever."

On the way back to his seat, Steven passed the father of the child, the child whom he had circumcised only five days earlier.

▪ In the Middle of the Night

Aside from the standard bedtime prayers, there is a custom to recite certain verses and psalms before going to sleep. One of these paragraphs is the beautiful chapter of Tehillim beginning with the words "Yoshev be'seser," a chapter which describes the security and confidence one can have in Hashem even in times of great danger. A recurring theme in the chapter is that of being under the shelter of Hashem; "I will say of Hashem, He is my shelter and fortress" and "beneath His wings you will be protected." Seldom do we stop to think of the implications of this idea.

The following story was told to me by its protagonist, who today lives in Atlanta, Georgia. It is an incident that he will never forget, and one that drove home to him this concept of "dwelling under the shelter of the Most High."

Just another springtime thunderstorm, thought Eli Melamed as he crawled exhaustedly into his bed. In the distance he could hear the thunder rumbling ominously as the storm approached, but it was not enough to keep him from his slumber. The week preceding Pesach is never a relaxing time in the average Jewish household, and for the 20-year-old student, this year was no exception. Since his family's move to the leafy northern suburbs of Atlanta, Georgia, it had been an uphill battle for the young man to adjust to life without the help of the two or three maids and servants he had become accustomed to in South Africa. Now, two days before the Festival of Freedom, he was feeling the effects of this reality, having been drafted into his mother's Pesach cleaning corps for the duration of the week. As Eli slept peacefully, the storm was rousing itself on the horizon.

It was a loud "clunk" on the roof which woke Eli in the early hours of the morning, and when he opened his eyes, the first thing he noticed was how the garden appeared to be permanently lit by successive bolts of lightning. Thunder boomed across the city and the wind howled dementedly through the tall Atlanta trees, driving torrents of rain against the windows of his room. After a moment of soporific deliberation, Eli hopped anxiously out of bed with the intention of informing his father of the unusual sound that had woken him. As he reached the door leading from his room into the hallway, a massive crashing, splintering sound ripped through his room behind him. Without looking back, he fled into the hall.

As Eli had slept peacefully, he had been blissfully unaware of the fact that one of the worst tornado systems in modern times was tearing through the United States. The same weather system that pummeled his home had raged across the southeastern section of the country, wreaking havoc and destruction throughout the states of Alabama, Mississippi, and Georgia. A long line of angry squalls accompanied by violent winds and baseball-sized hailstones lashed the countryside, overturning trucks and cars, uprooting trees, and reducing houses to pitiful heaps of rubble. When daylight eventually arrived, a horrific scene greeted the eyes of rescue workers and residents alike.

The worst damage occurred just west of Birmingham, Alabama, where a twister carved out a path a half-mile wide and 21 miles long, killing at least thirty people. Weather officials later confirmed that the twister had registered F-5 on the Fujita scale for measuring tornadoes, on which F-0 is the least intense and F-5 the most destructive. An F-5 tornado is very rare and carries winds in excess of 260 miles an hour.

After ripping its way through Alabama and Mississippi, the storm approached Georgia. An emergency worker who watched the wind overturn a woman's car in Cobb County later compared the scene to the aftermath of a massive bomb-blast. Deaths and damage occurred in widely scattered areas in Georgia, including Savannah in the southeastern part of the state and the northern suburbs of Atlanta more than 200 miles away.

When the final damage was tallied Thursday morning, it became apparent that the storm had claimed some 43 lives in the three states. Nearly 200 people were injured and over 2000 homes and businesses were either damaged or destroyed. Georgia had lost ten of its residents, two of them in the small suburb of Dunwoody.

Back in Dunwoody, Eli was standing in the hallway of his home, too bewildered to move, unsure of what to make of the thunderous noise which had moments before ripped through his room. When he finally dragged his sluggish mind out of what seemed to be a bizarre dream, he glanced at his watch, which showed that it was 1:30, and then continued down the hall to his father's room. Together, father and son cautiously approached Eli's room to assess what had indeed occurred.

They were greeted by a horrific sight. The room was unrecognizable. A massive, horizontal tree filled the entire room, with leaves and branches poking in all directions. Rain was pouring in and was gathering in small pools on the floor. Then their eyes came to rest on a terrifying sight, and both Eli and his father let out an audible gasp. The tree had come crashing through the roof, knocking down a section of the wall with it. Somehow the wall had slowed the tree's fall, and the massive trunk had come to a halt millimeters above the bed which Eli had been sleeping in moments earlier!

It was only when the storm abated and the first glimmers of dawn lit the garden that they were able to assess the extent of the damage. Outside, they found eleven other trees which had fallen toward the house domino-style, apparently causing the final tree to crash down onto Eli's bed. They also observed that the twelfth tree, Eli's tree, had been embedded in three feet of cement, which may very well have slowed its fall, allowing Eli enough time to move away from the bed and his room. Moreover, had the small branch not fallen onto the roof moments before the tree did, Eli would most certainly have been just another statistic of one of America's worst storms.

The next morning, the Melamed family set about *kashering* their kitchen for Pesach by means of a gas burner, the electricity lines having been severed by the falling trees. Fortunately, some good friends heard what had happened and invited the family not only for the *Sedarim* but for the entire Pesach week. As he sat the next night around the *Seder* table relieved and thankful, Eli was able to raise the four cups of wine with an entirely fresh perspective on the miraculous salvation that his forefathers had experienced in the middle of the night.

▪ Mother Prayer

The Talmud (Megillah 3a) teaches that focusing on Divine control of the world, by reciting Shema Yisrael, *can help avert harm.*

In Nefesh HaChaim *(3:12), R' Chaim of Volozhin states that a very effective way for a person to prevent others from harming him is to absolutely and completely concentrate on the fact that Hashem is the true G-d — there is no force other than Him, and He gives everything else its power.*

Let us meet a woman who did just that.

For days on end, heavy rains fell over the Natal highlands. It was as if someone had pulled a giant plug out of the sky, and the tons of water confined there had come tumbling down, intent on soaking the province to oblivion. Great torrents of water rushed down the hillsides, through towering forests, over narrow country roads, and through terrified little villages, sweeping tons of debris along with them in their headlong charge toward the sea. Rivers burst their banks, pulling down bridges and undermining roads. Giant trees floated majestically down the rivers like Spanish galleons amongst the flotsam and jetsam of hundreds of destroyed homes and farms. For a while it appeared as if the entire province would be washed inelegantly into the Indian Ocean.

After many days, the rains finally ceased. A shocked calm settled over the region as the inhabitants of Natal took stock of the damage and the farmers tallied their losses. The countryside seemed to gurgle with the sound of millions of gallons of water draining out of the soggy landscape. The rivers began to subside. It would be many days, if not weeks, however, before they returned to their normal levels.

The situation in Natal may have been bleak, but it was certainly not bleak enough to deter the Blackman family from making their biennial pilgrimage to the Drakansberg mountain range. Milton Blackman, a busy anesthesiologist practicing in Johannesburg, desperately needed a break from the stresses of the operating room; when the opportunity arose, not much would keep him and his wife Rhona from sharing their passion for the mountains with their young family. A few days after the rains subsided, they set out for the tranquil alpine resort of Injasuti in the central Drakansberg, threading their way through the valleys and over the high passes which crease the approach to South Africa's largest mountain range. As they neared their destination, the power of the floods became increasingly apparent to them. It was only when they found the bridge leading to the Injasuti resort lying shattered in the river it had once crossed, that they realized that their holiday plans were not completely waterproof. A hasty family discussion confirmed that no one was eager to turn back to Johannesburg, and they drove on in the hope of finding another retreat not obstructed by the flooded rivers. A short while later a sign indicated the route to a hotel called Dragon's Peak, and it was there that the Blackmans ended their wanderings and set about the always enjoyable task of relaxing and unwinding.

By the second day of their vacation the sun was once again shining brilliantly, almost as if to deny any involvement in the foul behavior of the preceding weeks. The glorious weather was all that was needed for the family to jump into their hiking boots, eager for some mountain air and the sound of scrunching underfoot. An early-morning ramble took them along the road out of the resort and over a small bridge which under normal circumstances crossed a narrow mountain stream. As a result of the flooding, however, the stream had swelled and had risen above the level of the bridge, forcing the group to wade through some six inches of water, much to the delight of the boys, Dovi, Yehoshua, and Gabi. The rest of their walk was uneventful, Milton's firm voice enough to keep his rambunctious brood on the straight and narrow. A couple of hours later they found themselves marching along the road back toward the resort. Once again they approached the submerged bridge, and again they proceeded to wade across it, boots in hand and feet enjoying the soothingly cool water.

Halfway across the bridge, Milton noticed that his eldest son, Dovi, had chosen to wade through the river itself on the upstream side of the bridge, instead of remaining on the road. A sharp reprimand from Milton brought the 11-year-old to his senses, and he moved toward the bridge to hoist himself up onto the road to join his family. By that time, Dovi was almost in the middle of the river and the top of the road reached to just below his chest height. He placed his hands onto the road and pushed downward in an attempt to lift himself onto the highway. Nothing happened. A look of concern flashed across his brow and it was quickly mirrored on the faces of his parents.

"Get on the bridge, Dovi," his mother blurted, half as an instruction and half out of fright.

"I can't, Ma; I'm stuck!" came the reply from the now panic-stricken boy.

Milton ran forward and began pulling the boy upward in the hope of dislodging him from whatever was pulling him down. Dovi would not budge.

Panic quickly turned to hysteria as the poor parents clung to their son, who was now slowly being pulled downward under the bridge.

It was only on a subsequent vacation that they discovered exactly what it was that had taken hold of their son. The road on which they stood had been built over a meandering mountain stream, which under normal circumstances would probably have been just a trickle of sparkling water. In order to allow the water to pass under the road, the road engineer had built it on a few large concrete pipes lying perpendicular to the direction of the road. On that fateful day, however, the trickle had swelled to a steady, silent torrent which rushed through the pipes under the road with remarkably strong pressure. Dovi's legs were being sucked into one of the concrete pipes.

The two parents dared not let their son go, and Dovi's younger brother Yehoshua was urgently dispatched to find help at the resort. As Milton clung to his son with his wife at his side, he looked into Dovi's eyes for what he was certain was the last time. Rhona began praying silently. Within minutes, Yehoshua was back with two men from the resort, one of whom immediately jumped into the water alongside the trapped boy. The man pulled and twisted as he attempted to free Dovi, but after a few minutes he climbed out of the water and apologized. "Can't be done," he declared morbidly. His colleague, dissatisfied with his friend's fateful prognosis, climbed down into the water to see what he could do. Moments later, he disappeared from view entirely, as if he had been but an apparition in the first place.

A lifetime passed. The man did not reappear. Either he was working on the trapped child under the water or else he too was now a victim of the powerful currents below. Rhona began praying aloud, trying to remember all the prayers she had been taught to invoke in times of dire need. Panic clenched her throat as she looked into her son's eyes.

Suddenly, she remembered a verse which she had learned years before, one which she had been told was a very powerful and meaningful verse (*Devarim* 4:35): "*Attah hareisa lada'as ki Hashem Hu ha'Elokim, ein od milvado*" — "You have been shown in order to know that Hashem, He is the G-d! There is none besides Him!" As she finished the sentence, there was a commotion in the water and the heroic helper, together with the stricken boy, came shooting out of the water, the man gasping deep gulps of fresh air.

When telling me his story, Milton added a chilling addendum. Years later a colleague of his who was a prominent member of the Johannesburg medical fraternity was also vacationing in the Drakansberg, when he found himself in exactly the same predicament as Dovi had been in many years before. This time, however, it was the father who was trapped and the sons who looked on. The story did not have a happy ending, and Milton related it only to put a perspective on the true danger to his son's life at the time, and how miraculous his survival was.

■ Lightning Response

Rambam, in his "Guide to the Perplexed," describes how night is a time when one's faith is tested, when one has to carry with him the knowledge and clarity he had during the day even though now it is completely dark. We live in a spiritual night. He compares our existence to a man stumbling across a wide plain during a fierce nighttime thunderstorm. He is completely surrounded by darkness, and is being constantly pounded by the storm. Suddenly the whole plain is lit up by a terrifying bolt of lightning. At that moment, the man can see his destination clearly, as well as the route he must take. But before he can look further, he is once again enveloped by the darkness. Now he must push on through the storm and the blackness, guiding himself with the memory of the clarity that he had moments before.

Similarly, a person stumbles through the darkness in life, often not seeing where he is going nor Who is in control of the world. Every now and then, however, there is a bolt of lightning, a moment of inspiration which allows him to see exactly how the world operates and Who it is that is in control. Then all goes dark again, and he must carry himself forward confidently with the memory of that inspiration, remembering as he does to open his eyes as the lightning flashes.

I had such an experience, and it came about through a real lightning bolt, on a strange Sunday afternoon.

"Sunny skies this Sunday mornin', folks," the radio announcer chirped cheerfully, "but if yesterday and Friday are anything to go by, it could be rainin' again in an hour. It's been four-seasons-in-a-day since the end o' last week."

It was a Sunday morning in the middle of November, and indeed the weather had been doing strange things. By November, the unique Highveld weather cycle has normally settled into its routine, and Johannesburg can generally expect sunny blue skies most of the day followed by abrupt and dramatic thunderstorms in the late afternoon, which drench the city in a few short minutes and then disappear as suddenly as they arrived. For the few days prior to that Sunday, however, the weather had been unusually erratic: cold and drizzly, then hot for a few hours, then cold again.

Sunday is my weekly Hatzalah slot, the day on which I lug around a cellular telephone and a two-way radio as the dispatcher for this remarkable volunteer paramedic organization. It's also a day typically punctuated by phone calls from people who say things like, "Huloooo, is Eddie there please?" followed by a confused apology for misdialing.

On this particular Sunday, I was once again on duty, and after sending out the standard test call in the morning, I set about my daily chores. The phone was quiet the entire morning, until 1:03 in the afternoon when it rang for the first time that day.

It was an elderly lady, who informed me that her husband, an equally elderly and very ill man, needed to be transported to a local hospital by ambulance. She insisted, however, that it was not an emergency and that she only needed assistance in arranging the ambulance. When I pressed her a bit, though, she conceded that it might be worthwhile to send out one or two volunteers to assist with the transfer into the ambulance, as her husband was not always fully rational and tended to be obstinate at times. I immediately called for an ambulance, and then dispatched a call to all responders, asking for two volunteers to assist with the transfer.

Ten seconds later, my radio squawked into life: "Gili responding," bleeleeleeleep …

Followed almost immediately by: "Gidon here, three minutes away," bleeleeleeleep …

I called the woman again, and informed her that two men would be at her residence within the ensuing three minutes, as well as an ambulance shortly thereafter. A minute later the radio went on again with "Gili on scene," bleeleeleeleep…

The time was 1:05 p.m.

Two minutes later, I was getting back to my work when the radio burst into life once again.

"This is Gili to dispatch, Gili to dispatch, this patient is in respiratory distress! Please upgrade to Priority One NOW!" bleeleeleeleep ...

I fumbled with the phone, dialed, recorded a shaky message informing the responders of the latest development, and then at the instruction of the electronic voice, pressed 2 to send. Instantly, twenty-five phones burst into life around town, for the second time in ten minutes.

1:08 — "Gidon on the scene"... bleeleeleeleep ... Antoine and Arnie on the way."

The voices were controlled but slightly frayed at the edges. Within ten minutes, five highly qualified responders were at the scene. For the next fifteen minutes, my radio was silent, and in my mind, I visualized the men calmly assessing the patient, supplying oxygen, and stabilizing him for transport to the hospital. When the distant wail of the ambulance siren reached my ears, I radioed the scene and informed them of its progress, predicting its arrival within two to three minutes. Sure enough, a few moments later my radio crackled: "Arnie to dispatch, ambulance on scene." I breathed a sigh of relief, and as the tension drained away, I headed for my desk to fill out the report forms. The time was 1:36 p.m.

The sky had darkened outside, and after a minute of writing I reached up to turn on a lamp. A storm was brewing. Suddenly there was a flash of light followed almost immediately by a rolling thunderclap. I was about to get up to close my window, when the phone rang.

"Hatzalah medical rescue, do you have an emergency?"

"You guys better come quick! Lightning's struck someone up here, Jewish Guild Country Club, top of Sylvia Pass —"

I cut him off before he could finish his sentence. I had all the details I needed and I knew that time was of the essence. I gripped the phone and dialed. At the tone, I recorded a terse message, then pressed 2 to send. I held the radio in my other hand and waited for what felt like an eternity. Then —

"Brian responding with Antoine, we're six minutes away ..." bleeleeleeleep ...

I could hear the siren in the background as he spoke, his voice terse, urgent.

"Daniel, f-f-f-five minutes ..." bleeleeleeleep ...

They all knew this was a big one, the one everyone dreaded, and their voices wavered slightly as they spoke.

"Ryan en route, six minutes ..." bleeleeleeleep ... "Vaughn, 7 minutes ..." bleeleeleeleep ...

The storm broke. While I dialed the local private ambulance service for backup, seven Hatzalah cars were already roaring and slithering through the suddenly flooded streets, drivers clutching their steering wheels tightly, praying that their tires would grip the road so as not to create yet another emergency scene. The dispatcher of the private ambulance company I called sounded librarianly calm, her tension only showing when she informed me that her vehicles were traveling as fast as possible, but were being inhibited because the roads were "wettery and slip."

I glanced at my watch. It read 1:41 p.m. The lightning struck at 1:38, and I knew that if the man's heart had indeed arrested, he would not last for much longer. From my seat at the desk, I heard the sirens wailing in the distance.

The phone rang. It was the man who had placed the call, wanting to know where the paramedics were. I told him that they were on their way, and used the opportunity to glean some further information. He told me that there were in fact two casualties, but that only one was unconscious. I wrote down a few further details, finished the call, and then relayed the updated information over the radios. I waited for what felt like an hour.

1:45 — "Daniel on scene ..." bleeleeleeleep ..."Brian and Antoine on scene ..." bleeleeleeleep ...

1:46 — "Ryan on scene ..." bleeleeleeleep ... "Arnie on scene ..." bleeleeleeleep ...

Suddenly: "WE HAVE ONE FULL RE-SUS! I REPEAT, ONE FULL RE-SUS!" bleeleeleeleep...

It was the slightly shaky voice of Brian, who had assessed the patients, and was informing the team that one patient was in fact clinically dead, and needed to be resuscitated if he was to live. I gripped the radio tighter. Silence reigned for yet another lifetime.

1:51 — "Daniel to dispatch, ambulance on scene … Kramer's also on scene …" bleeleeleeleep …

My adrenalin-charged mind attempted to visualize the scene. Ventilator bagging, heart massage, defibrillator paddles. After a minute I gave up imagining and began saying *Tehillim*. For me, as the dispatcher, the period after the arrival of the team on the scene is always the hardest. Everyone present is usually occupied, and there is seldom someone to keep "dispatch" updated with the patient's progress. You've done all you can anyway, and there is nothing to do but wait for further orders.

I began pacing the house, glancing at my watch every few seconds, willing its frail hands to stop their interminable march. The storm had abated a few minutes after the initial call, and the sky was beginning to brighten. I walked to the window and gazed in the direction of Sylvia Pass, once again trying to imagine what was unfolding only a kilometer or two away. Suddenly, I heard a faint whoppity-whoppity sound, and my hopes began to rise. As the form of a tiny helicopter rose over the horizon and grew to full size it banked sharply in the direction of the Country Club. I had to hold myself back from cheering loudly. Someone on the scene had obviously ordered a chopper, and it could only mean that there was someone alive to be transported. The time was 2:10 p.m.

Twenty minutes later, an elated Brian was on the radio to announce that both patients were stable and en route to a nearby clinic. The man who had been directly hit by lightning had been downgraded from Priority Four, a euphemistic term for dead, to Priority One. Thanks to the quick response of the team, and the marvels of the defibrillator, the 76-year-old man had survived a direct strike of lightning — hundreds of kilovolts. He was regaining consciousness as the helicopter climbed into the air and headed for the hospital.

As the adrenalin high slowly settled, I began to review the events of the hour, and was suddenly overcome with a feeling of astonishment at the amazing synchronicity which had occurred. Purely by coincidence, the two calls of the day had come within a half-hour of one another, the first call ending with the arrival of the ambulance, less than *two minutes* before the lightning strike. Had it been the other way around, who knows what those extra minutes might have meant.

The next day I was informed that two foreign workers were killed in an identical incident in the very same storm some two kilometers away. On that Sunday with the strange weather, it was obvious that someone was being looked after.

Postscript: The elderly man recovered well after his brush with death, and was talking and even mobile a short while afterwards. Unfortunately, his condition deteriorated subsequently, and a few months later he passed away. This turn of events does not in any way diminish the significance of his miraculous resuscitation, for it is one of the fundamentals of Judaism that a single minute of life is infinitely valuable. This too is one of the founding principles of an organization like Hatzalah, and highlights the importance and eternal value of the selfless commitment of all of those involved in this remarkable organization.

▪ Family Simchah

Twice a day after our silent Amidah, *we recite the* Tachanun *prayer in which we bury our head in our arm, and beseech Hashem to have mercy on us despite our unworthiness. There are certain occasions, however, when this prayer is not recited, joyous times which do not suit the nature of this prayer. One such instance is when there is present in the synagogue a man who has been married within the preceding seven days. What is fascinating to note about this law is that as a result of this man's* simchah, *the entire congregation does not say* Tachanun, *including visitors who might never even have met the groom. This reveals a fascinating insight into our attitude toward what the world at large refers to as "coincidence." Two men have had a rendezvous in time — the groom who is celebrating one of the most significant moments in his life, and the visitor who just happened to be passing through on that day. Indeed there are no coincidences in life, and it is clear that their paths have crossed for a reason. For that short moment, the visitor has entered the groom's world and is celebrating with him.*

The following extraordinary story concerns a distant relative of mine and describes a momentary rendezvous between two people, with far-reaching consequences.

Philip and Eva Kringel desperately wanted a second child. It had been five years since the birth of their daughter Tanya, and since then, Eva had not been blessed with another child. The middle-aged couple was certain that a second child would be the perfect way to transform them from a threesome into a family, yet it seemed that it was not meant to be. After careful deliberation, they eventually decided to investigate the possibility of adopting a baby.

Since their arrival in Seattle, Washington from Cape Town, Philip and Eva had seen only success. The clinic where Philip worked was constantly at the cutting edge of technology, pioneering methods for remote consultations with patients in outlying locations, a project which earned Philip a few moments of glory on national television. Their daughter Tanya was thriving in the nearby Jewish day school, so much so that she became distressed every time the school year was interrupted by holidays. Her shared passion with her father for the outdoors allowed them to spend many quality hours together, exploring the mountains and parks surrounding their hometown. Now the time had come for the family to expand, and Philip and Eva began to set the wheels in motion. They placed calls to various adoption agencies and filled out the necessary forms. Then they began the long and tedious process of waiting, and waiting and waiting.

After eighteen frustrating months, the couple's prayers were finally answered. Wayne Seth was born in March 2001, in Dallas, Texas, and twelve hours after his delivery his new parents were cradling him lovingly in their arms. Eva and Philip remained in Dallas for a week to conclude the details of the adoption before bringing their long-awaited bundle of happiness into their own home. Philip described how the little baby brought only joy from the outset. He loved his food (a habit which he apparently picked up quickly from his new father), and was sleeping twelve hours at night (a habit which he apparently picked up quickly from his new mother). At first, little Tanya was quite put out by the sudden arrival of her new sibling, but she soon got used to not being the center of attention. As Wayne developed and matured into a lively toddler, the two started getting along and played together constantly.

A short while after little Wayne's arrival, Philip placed a phone call, a phone call which was to change his life. The call was motivated by an experience he had had during the frustrating months that they had waited for Wayne.

Eva and Philip had decided that while waiting for news of their application, it was probably worth their while to attend various workshops and meetings on the subject of adoption. They figured that it would be useful to hear what other parents had been through and what they could expect if their search proved fruitful. It was at one such meeting that Philip was deeply moved, a feeling which eventually led him to make that fateful phone call.

Philip had always known that he, too, was adopted. He had been born in Cape Town and was raised there by his loving foster parents, Selma and Joe Kringel. The fact that he was adopted had never been an issue for him, and he loved his foster parents and had always felt loved by them. Philip had never felt the desire to seek out his biological parents or learn more about them. Then one evening, he was sitting together with Eva in a forum on the subject of adoption, when a woman stood up. The woman told of how she had once given up a child for adoption, and how to that very day knew nothing of his whereabouts or what had become of him. A second mother stood up after her and echoed the same story.

Philip and Eva were very moved by the women's tales. Subsequent to that meeting, Philip made two resolutions. First, with the help of his wife, he resolved to meet the birth mother of any child they adopted, so that they could answer any questions the child might have in the future. Furthermore, after much thought, Philip decided to set about the daunting task of tracking down his own biological parents.

It was only after the arrival of Wayne Seth in their home that Philip mustered up the courage to make the call. At the time of the adoption, Philip had been further moved by the love which little Wayne's mother had shown for the child, and by the fact that she was still able to follow through with the adoption, providing Philip and Eva with the opportunity and privilege of raising her child. Philip had suddenly gained a new appreciation for the people who had brought him into the world forty years earlier, and felt a sudden need to meet them, at least to say an awkward "thank you." The call was a long-distance one to an adoption agency in South Africa, a call which set into motion a chain of events which was to change Philip's life forever.

From the call and the subsequent correspondence, Philip learned that his birthparents, Max and Lynette Silberg, still lived in Cape Town. He had been born when his parents were very young, and had been given up for adoption because they felt that they were not ready to raise a child properly. Then came the bombshell that Philip had never dreamed of. According to the agency, two years after Philip was given up for adoption, Max and Lynette had another child, Steven, followed by a daughter Lisa and a second son Saul. Incredibly, Philip, in the course of a few hours, had discovered that he had two full blood-brothers, as well as one full blood-sister, whom he'd known nothing about for close to forty years!

The ensuing days were a whirlwind of emotions and feelings for Philip as he got to know more about his family, whom he had been oblivious of for so long. He learned that his brother Steven still resided in Cape Town with a wife and two small children. His little sister Lisa was living in Los Angeles, while his baby brother Saul had been in London for five years. The shock was not limited to Philip, though, for none of his siblings had been aware of his existence either. Within days Philip had made contact with his brothers and sister, and they began to communicate regularly.

A month after their incredible discovery, Philip's sister Lisa together with her daughter Mandy traveled from Los Angeles to Seattle to spend a few days with her long-lost brother and his family. It was a memorable weekend, and both Philip and Eva testified to the fact that they had never met someone with whom they felt so comfortable and so natural so quickly. The physical similarities between them were definitely visible, and their respective children were inseparable for the entire weekend. They traded stories and related anecdotes of the separate lives that they had lived in such close proximity to one another while they were both still in Cape Town. They relived the happy moments and the sad, and before long felt a close bond developing between them. At one point during that weekend, Philip and Eva described to Lisa one of the most special moments in their lives, their wedding which they had celebrated while still in Cape Town. As Philip spoke, a strange look came over Lisa's face and she suddenly sat bolt upright. She paled slightly and then stammered: "You're not going to believe this —" she hesitated, "but I think I was at your wedding!"

To a dumbfounded brother and sister-in-law, Lisa described how, many years before, she had been dating a man who had invited her to accompany him to a cousin's wedding. The man's name was Charles Maizel, whom Eva remembered being at the wedding. Eva was unable, however, to remember who had accompanied him. Suddenly Philip had an idea. With rising excitement and a bit of trepidation, Philip dug out the video from their wedding and gingerly placed the cassette in the machine. The tension was palpable as Philip, Eva, and Lisa waited to see what they would find. As the images began to flit across the screen, the three of them felt multiple cold shivers running up and down their spines. Sure enough, the sister whom Philip had not known even existed was present at his wedding, and by some freak "coincidence" she appeared in most of the scenes in the video!

Thanks to the selflessness of the Kringels who were willing to adopt a young baby in need, a chain of events was set into motion which eventually united Philip with his family and the sister whom he had never met before — at least not consciously. Moreover, by an incredible stroke of *hashgachah pratis*, Lisa was given the opportunity of celebrating at her brother's wedding, even though she was oblivious at the time to the fact that he was even related to her.

▪ Commander in Chief

For those who are fearful of flying, there is no doubt that there are specific moments during a flight which are more terrifying than others. When the aircraft is cruising peacefully at altitude and the lights are dim, even the most sensitive flyers normally are calm. It is when the captain encourages his passengers over the loudspeaker to fasten their seat belts that heart rates begin to climb, and it is when the craft shudders through a patch of turbulence that the blood begins to drain away from people's faces.

R' Nachum Cohen, a regular visitor to Johannesburg, often likes to point out that when the seat beneath one begins to buck and jerk, one's reaction is to tighten the seat belt and pray harder. It would never cross one's mind to rush to the flight deck to offer one's assistance, for there is a basic understanding that the man sitting behind the controls is eminently more qualified to handle the situation than anyone else aboard the craft.

This situation is highly symbolic of life, for all too often, we feel the world around us shudder, and we are tempted to "rush to the front" to check whether the "Pilot" is aware of what is going on. We must remind ourselves that the "Pilot" of this existence is infinitely more qualified to handle the situation. We must just fasten our figurative seat belts and do whatever is in our hands to do. Even in the heat of the moment, when things seem out of control, we must remember that in fact everything is being supervised.

Everything is under control.

The following story was related to me by family friends.

In the deeper recesses of his consciousness, he was only vaguely aware of the jaunty notes being played by the five-piece band. The festivities around him seemed abstract, removed, as if he was contemplating the scene through the wrong end of a telescope. A young man floated past, champagne glass delicately poised in his hand, his eyes twinkling as if reflecting the merriment in the air. Morris's mind was on another continent, halfway around the world, where he had left his family so that he could attend this wedding. It was one of those sacrifices one only makes for a best friend. His eyes misted over as he stared at the candle burning steadily in the center of the silver-bedecked table. He felt a pricking behind his eyelids, and only when something splashed onto his hand did he realize that he was crying.

The sun which had just set over the celebration in the United States was rising on the other side of the globe, ready to cast its rays on another difficult day for Morris's tiny, innocent, and very ill son. Daniel had been born ten long months earlier with a genetic disorder which had left him with many midline deformities. Of these maladies, the most life-threatening was the fact that he aspirated when he swallowed, which resulted in his suffering from chronic pneumonia. The first ten months of his fragile life were spent in and out of the sterile wards of Johannesburg's hospitals as the doctors tried everything in their power to help the young child. No medical man in South Africa was prepared to recommend corrective surgery; even the experts concurred that the child was too small to undergo any major procedure. Daniel's exhausted parents could only pray for a miracle.

Of the diverse guests attending the celebration, Morris found himself sitting next to perhaps one of the most unusual visitors one could expect to find at a Jewish wedding. Although the absence of a feather headdress made him hard to distinguish from any of the other revelers, Morris's neighbor happened to be the chief of the Mohegan tribe, a Native American group originating from a similar part of the continent as the Iroquois.

Morris's tears attracted the attention of the chief. Sensing that comfort was of more value than words, he draped a comforting arm over Morris's shoulder and waited silently for the tears to subside. When Morris finally looked up, he found a concerned pair of eyes looking down into his own. Behind those soft eyes Morris sensed that there lay an understanding and caring heart, and when the chief finally inquired what it was that was troubling him, ten months of anxiety and sorrow came tumbling out. Morris described his little son's situation and the predicament he and his wife Rene found themselves in as parents, trying to alleviate the suffering of their innocent infant.

The chief listened compassionately to Morris's tale of woe, taking in every detail. When Morris had finished, the chief stroked his chin thoughtfully. Finally, he spoke. "This may come as a surprise to you," he began, "but I understand your predicament in its entirety. You see, I have a grandchild who has a very similar problem." Morris stared at him in disbelief. "We had some very successful surgery done," continued the chief, "by a surgeon in Hartford, Connecticut, who is a pediatric gastroenterologist."

Morris's face lit up as a warm shaft of hope pierced his heart. Before he had a chance to release the flood of questions bursting from his head, the chief's voice took on a businesslike tone: "I'm booking you an appointment to see him either tomorrow or the next day. Get yourself over there and see what he has to say."

The fax lines between South Africa and the United States transferred Daniel's medical information across the Atlantic, as Rene rushed to supply the surgeon with the data he might need for the in-abstentia consultation. After seeing the records and discussing Daniel's case history with Morris, the surgeon recommended a series of specialized tests to be done in South Africa, on the basis of which a treatment plan could be mapped out.

As Morris winged his way back toward the African continent, he contemplated the events of the past few days. An icy chill coursed through his body as he pieced together the links binding the chain of events together, which had eventually led to a breakthrough for Daniel. It had all started with his close friendship, which had led to his journey of self-sacrifice, his out-of-character tears which had led to his conversation with the improbable Indian chief, which had finally led them to just the man who was needed to heal his son.

■　　　■　　　■

Two weeks later, Daniel was wheeled into an operating room at the Linksfield clinic in Johannesburg for major stomach surgery. Based on the recommendations of the Hartford surgeon, a gastrointestinal tube was to be fitted to Daniel's stomach to avoid reflux. Outside the entrance of the operating room, his parents paced wearily back and forth, reciting *Tehillim* and trying not to think about what was happening to their son on the other side of the doors. When the surgeon finally appeared in the waiting room, relief flooded over them even before the doctor had a chance to utter a word. The glow on his face blurted out to Morris and Rene that the surgery had gone well. The journey was far from over, but they had reached the first milestone.

Five days after the operation, Rene lay dozing in a vacant hospital bed near her tiny son. Daniel slept peacefully in a crib by her side. It was *Motza'ei Shabbos*, and Morris had slipped out for a bit of a break from the draining environment of the hospital to spend some time with a friend who was visiting from out of town. All was peaceful. At 10:30, a nurse tapped her gently on the shoulder and Rene woke with a start. She looked up to find a policeman standing awkwardly next to the night nurse. "There's been an accident, ma'am," he stammered, "your husband — you'd better come down to the emergency room."

This is what had happened a few minutes earlier:

On the other side of town, in a suburb called Bramley, Morris pulled into the driveway of the home where his friend was staying. He had phoned him earlier and invited him out for coffee. After spending so many difficult hours in the hospital with Daniel it would be a welcome change to chat with an old friend for a while. The front door of the house slammed, and his friend hopped into the passenger seat. They greeted each other warmly. Morris shifted to reverse and slowly backed out of the driveway.

Suddenly he became aware of a shadowy figure standing next to the car. His eyes scanned the darkness, trying to understand what the intruder wanted. A stab of fear ran through his stomach as he discerned a black object in the man's hand. A large gun was aimed directly at his window! A carjacking! In an instant, Morris's reflexes took over, and he floored the gas pedal. The car hurtled backward toward the street and away from the gun. Suddenly the entire world seemed to erupt as the hijackers opened fire on the receding car. Glass exploded all around the two friends as the hail of bullets smashed through the windows.

A searing pain sliced into Morris's arm. When he looked over at his friend he saw blood coursing from his friend's face as well as a red stain quickly growing at his midriff. Adrenalin coursed through his veins as he slammed the car into drive with his uninjured arm and roared out of the line of fire. The car hesitated for what seemed like a lifetime before the wheels finally gripped the pavement and pulled the car away. Morris knew all too well that although they were safely away from the bullets, their biggest enemy now was loss of blood. He urgently pointed the car in the direction of the Linksfield clinic, a route which he knew all too well, and let the adrenalin take over. Five minutes later, he screeched into the clinic parking lot.

Rene got down to the emergency room as her husband and his friend were being examined by the doctors on call. Morris had been hit in the left arm, the bullet completely shattering the elbow joint. His heroic and instantaneous reaction had saved the life of his friend who miraculously survived a bullet to the jaw and stomach. Morris underwent surgery on his arm, and later a bone graft to restore function to the joint. Once again, the dust settled and the story seemed to be drawing to a close.

A few months later, however, it took a terrifying twist.

Morris and Rene were invited to a *simchah* and Morris decided to wear the same suit that he had been wearing on the night of the shooting. The jacket had been cleaned and the hole in the arm repaired. Pushing his hand into the pocket, he was surprised to feel something hard. He removed the jacket, pulled open the lining, and discovered to his horror a shiny bullet. On closer examination he and Rene discovered a small hole in the center of his jacket, directly in line with his heart! Contrary to what they'd thought, there had been more than one bullet. This second bullet had penetrated the outer layer of his lined jacket but had somehow not been able to penetrate any further! It was truly a miracle.

Incidentally, his friend who was also injured had stopped keeping kosher a short while before the incident. He was struck by two bullets, one to the mouth and one to the stomach. Thankfully, he has since then fully recovered from his injuries.

▪ Triumph Over Adversity

We read in the Haggadah of Pesach how the great Sage Rabbi Yehudah coined an acrostic for the Ten Plagues, using the first letter of each plague, Detz"ach Ada"sh Be"achav. The underlying meaning of this seemingly simplistic teaching is that each group of plagues was intended to teach a fundamental principle to the Egyptians and anyone who chooses to follow in their evil ways.

The second set was made up of the plagues of wild beasts, pestilence, and boils. The purpose of this set was to confound the notion prevalent among the Egyptians that although there may be a Creator Who oversees the general running of the world, He nevertheless pays no attention to the individual lives of the human species. The consequence of this outlook was a belief that the experiences of life are completely random, and that no distinction exists between those people who serve Hashem and those who do not. These three plagues demonstrated, unequivocally, that every single detail of each human being's life is ordained on High, that every experience which confronts us in this world to this very day is measured and tailored exclusively for the person concerned, and is a consequence of his or her actions. All three of these plagues should have struck every person in the country equally, yet they were selective. All three only struck the Egyptian citizens, while the Jews were unharmed (Kli Yakar).

The message of the second set of plagues is one that must be constantly reinforced, even for G-d-fearing people. We have to remember that not only is there an infinitely powerful Creator, but that He concerns Himself with the daily lives of His people. The following inspiring story was told to me by a close family friend.

No young person leaves school without a dream. Some dream of achieving fame and fortune, others have the ambition of traveling the world, some even hope to change it. It is probably a dangerous combination of large doses of young optimism, coupled with a healthy helping of newfound freedom, which fuels these ambitions. Whatever their source may be, few are spared from these fantasies.

Jeff Saitowitz wanted a car — but not just any car. From the day he left school, Jeff dreamed of owning a Triumph Spitfire. He could not quite put his finger on what it was exactly that made him weak in the knees every time he saw one drive by. It probably had something to do with the tiny soft-top's character, a small item with a big engine, characteristics which Jeff himself seemed to share.

In 1969, when he was only a few years out of school, Jeff realized his dream through dedication and focus, and became the proud owner of a souped-up convertible Triumph Spitfire Mk 2 in pearl white. The car had everything he had dreamed of: double exhausts, wide tires, fast-release hand brake, and more horses under the hood than one could hope to find under the saddles of all the cowboys to have ever roamed the Wild West. Jeff was one proud young man and the envy of all his friends.

Unfortunately his joyful existence was short lived. Not long after his twenty-third birthday, a knock on the front door heralded the arrival of a member of the South African Police Service, who bluntly informed Jeff's mother that her husband had died suddenly while walking in the street in Central Johannesburg. Shattered by the devastating tragedy, the family was left reeling by the abruptness with which it had struck. It was Jeff's mom, however, who was hardest hit. His parents had enjoyed an unusually close and intense marriage, and after hearing of her life partner's sudden passing, Mrs. Saitowitz's health deteriorated drastically. She suffered a sudden debilitating asthma attack and was admitted to the hospital.

Mrs. Saitowitz had been an asthma sufferer for many years and had been on a regimen of medication to prevent such attacks, but the trauma and grief surrounding her husband's passing had been too much for the poor elderly woman. By early 1970 her life was slipping away and every day that her lung function deteriorated, Jeff and his younger sister's prayers were intensified. Losing one parent was tragic enough; losing both parents in one year was almost more than they could handle.

Despite the upheaval and trauma at home and the increased responsibility placed on his young shoulders, Jeff made a point of attending a *minyan* three times a day, so that he could recite *Kaddish* for his father, as is customary for a mourner to do during the first year after the passing of a close relative. He was employed at the time by a large hospital group in the center of town, and every day after work he would reroute his way home via a synagogue in the suburb of Yeoville, a thirty-minute drive through heavy traffic, for *Minchah* and *Ma'ariv* prayers. Every so often, when the traffic was too congested and it appeared that its owner might miss his *minyan*, the little white sports coupe would break free from the line of cars and would head to the Ponevezh shul in Doornfontein, which happened to be closer than Jeff's preferred *minyan* in Yeoville.

The Ponevezh shul was established in the 1920's by the early settlers in Doornfontein, who came from Ponevezh in Europe, a town later made famous by the illustrious yeshivah which bears its name. The stalwarts of Ponevezh seemed to Jeff to be relics of a previous eon. It struck him that membership appeared only to be granted to the bearer of a walking cane, the proud wearer of a pair of hearing aids, or the owner of a head of white hair. In short, Ponevezh made Jeff feel something like the only guy in a suit and tie at an informal party, and for that reason it was never his first choice for a place in which to *daven*. He was usually number eleven anyway.

Not long after Jeff started periodically popping into Ponevezh, one of its elderly congregants sadly returned to his Maker in a pedestrian accident while crossing the road to get to the synagogue. The next time Jeff turned up at the shul he was cornered by nine old men who demanded that he become their full-time tenth. Thus he became a member of the Ponevezh *minyan*. Within a few weeks he was commissioned as the permanent *chazan*, he became the *minyan's* youthful mascot, and he even began speaking a hesitant Yiddish. Jeff was most popular, however, because of his brash little motorcar, and each day after *Shacharis*, the old men would squabble over whose chance it was to get a ride home with him, in the sleek new vehicle.

The condition of his mother deteriorated, and Jeff began to lose hope. The hospital had informed them that there was nothing more they could do for the ailing woman, and she had returned home despondent. In desperation, Jeff consulted with the doctors he came across during the course of his work. After numerous inquiries, he was informed that there was a certain doctor, Dr. Ivan Kalminowitz, who had been tremendously successful in treating chronic asthma. His methods were allegedly rather unconventional, but having exhausted all other avenues, Jeff resolved to make an appointment with the doctor posthaste.

It was a Monday morning when he placed the call to the doctor's office. He described his mother's dire situation to the nurse who answered the call, and begged her for the next available appointment. After making him hold for a few seconds, she returned to the phone and informed him in her most clinical voice that the next available appointment with the doctor was some four months away. The doctor spends much time with each of his patients, she informed him, and he cannot treat more than a few each day. Her words cut through him like a scalpel as he replaced the phone in its cradle and slumped his head on the desk. He knew all too well that his mother would never survive the four months until Dr Kalminowitz could see her.

The rest of that day he walked around in a gloomy depression. His hands were tied. He felt so powerless, so incapable of doing anything for his poor elderly mother. As he drove toward the Ponevezh shul that afternoon he contemplated the futility of all things material in the face of such hardships. What was his dream car worth when his life was turning into such a nightmare? That afternoon his prayers were for his mother.

Because the *minyan* consisted of only ten men, a visitor didn't usually go unnoticed, but that evening, Jeff was so preoccupied with his woes that he almost failed to notice an unfamiliar man praying with them. It was only when he got to the final *Mourner's Kaddish* of *Ma'ariv* that he realized that someone was reciting the *Kaddish* along with him. After completing the prayers Jeff approached the stranger, and on hearing that the man had *yahrtzeit,* wished him the traditional "long life."

As he went out to his car a few moments later, Jeff observed the newcomer examining his little Spitfire with interest. "Nice wheels," said the man, his voice unsuccessful in concealing his genuine admiration for the little coupe's lines. "Thank you," replied Jeff cheerfully, always ready to accept a compliment on behalf of his new car. Parked behind his Spitfire, Jeff noticed, was a brand-new Dodge gleaming in the shadows, obviously belonging to his newfound admirer. He realized that the stranger had to be someone important; the Dodge was a top-of-the-line model and even had a telephone installed, something very unusual and exclusive at the time. The man offered his hand. Jeff grasped it and introduced himself. What happened next shook him to the core and will stay with him for as long as he lives.

The stranger introduced himself. "Hi, Ivan Kalminowitz's the name, Dr. Ivan Kalminowitz if you wish to be formal. My office is just around the corner. I had *yahrtzeit* tonight and I wasn't going to make it home in time for my regular *minyan* in Cyrildene, so I popped in here instead. Rather quaint old place, don't you think?"

When Jeff finally managed to find his tongue again, he couldn't hold himself back, and the days and weeks of frustration came pouring out to the doctor he thought he would never meet. Unable to hold back the tears, he told the doctor all about his father's passing and how his mother had taken ill. He described how the hospital had all but given up on her, and how she was lying in their apartment in Yeoville waiting to die. He then told the now-startled doctor how he had tried to make an appointment to see him, but the nurse had put him off. The doctor listened carefully and then, without waiting to hear the end of the story, he said, "What are we waiting for? Today I will be your passenger." They hopped into Jeff's little car and roared off towards Jeff's apartment and his ailing mother.

Jeff recounts how the words of the doctor as he entered his mother's room are permanently etched in his memory to this very day. Jeff's mother, gasping for breath, told the doctor about her husband's untimely death and informed him that she had reached the end of the road. She told him that she could hardly breathe and that life was unbearable. In a most compassionate voice, the doctor said to her: "Don't worry, Mrs. Saitowitz, we will make you better — and then we'll find you another husband!"

Within a short amount of time Dr. Kalminowitz, using his very unconventional methods and a carefully monitored diet, had Mrs. Saitowitz's asthma under control. She recovered completely and merited to see her children married off and her first grandchildren born. Although Dr. Kalminowitz never kept the second half of his promise in finding her a husband, he did become a close friend of the Saitowitz family, and their friendship remains fast to this day.

And all because of an old shul — and a small car — in Doornfontein.

▪ Marriage Visa

A certain wealthy woman once challenged the Sage Rabbi Yosi bar Chalafta:

"In how many days did Hashem create His world?" she wanted to know.

Replied Rabbi Yosi: "[He created it] in six days, as it is written: 'In six days, Hashem made the heavens and the earth.' "

Said the woman: " And from then until now, what does He do?"

To which Rabbi Yosi answered: "Hashem sits and pairs up partners. The daughter of X to Y, the wife of A to B, the money of Y to Z."

"And this is His occupation?" she retorted brazenly. "Even I can do that! I have many servants and maids," she said, "and in no time at all I will match them up [as husbands and wives]."

Replied the Sage: "It may be easy for you [to match them up], but for Hashem it is as difficult as the splitting of the Sea of Reeds!"

After Rabbi Yosi departed, the woman gathered together one thousand menservants and one thousand maidservants, and she lined them up in long rows. She then walked along the rows, gesturing from side to side and declaring "you for her," "you for him," and "you for her." In one night she had paired up all two thousand of them.

The next morning servants began arriving en masse at her door, one with a wounded head, another with an injured eye, and a third with a broken leg. When she inquired what had happened, the maidservants all told her, "I don't want him," and the menservants all said, "I don't want her."

The woman immediately sent for Rabbi Yosi bar Chalafta and declared in front of him: "There is no G-d like yours; your Torah is true, pleasant, and praiseworthy" (Bereishis Rabbah 68).

Divine matchmaking is truly an awe-inspiring occupation, for two entirely separate destinies must be honed and directed for many years before they can come together and merge into one. What follows is a case in point, as described to me by the person concerned.

Buenos Aires, the capital city of Argentina, lies on the east coast of South America, where the Rio de la Plata flows into the Atlantic Ocean. Named for the fair winds or "Buenos Aires" which favor her wide port, it was here that many Jews fled in the early 1900's ahead of the inferno which subsequently engulfed Europe. Most arrived with little to their names. Some quickly found fame and fortune, while for others the fair winds of their new homeland heralded little more than poverty and hardship.

Norman Millner was born shortly after the war to Lithuanian parents in the city of Buenos Aires. His parents had arrived in Argentina shortly before the war, hoping to start their lives afresh. Unfortunately, they never really recovered from the financial upheaval of shifting continents, and the family remained destitute for the majority of Norman's youth. Norman was brought up as a completely secular Jew and was sent to a left-wing Jewish day school with strong antireligious leanings. Emphasis was placed on the Yiddish language, which was seen as the vehicle for Jewish identity and uniqueness even in place of Zionism, an outlook strongly subscribed to by Norman's father. Times were tough for the Millners and little money was available for youthful entertainment. At age 12 Norman was even sent to a holiday camp for impoverished Jewish children, run by a nonreligious left-wing organization (see the following story). Then, in 1963, his childhood came to an abrupt end with the passing of his father. Norman was only 15 at the time. From then on, things did not get easier for the Millners; the small family had lost their breadwinner and Norman's mother had to struggle to support herself and her son. Norman wanted to help but employment prospects for him proved significantly bleak because he was very young and lacked qualifications or experience in any particular field.

Then one day in early 1964, they received a call from an uncle of his, who was living in South Africa. The South African Jewish community, unlike the Argentinean one, is made up of a large proportion of Lithuanian émigrés. Thus when the Millners moved from Lithuania to the predominantly Polish Argentina, some of their relatives chose to settle in South Africa instead. Norman's uncle had a proposal. Let the young man come to South Africa for a year, he said, where he will learn to speak English. With a second language Norman will be far more employable and will be able to support the family when he returns to Argentina, he reasoned. Thus Norman ended up on the other side of the Atlantic, where he still resides today and runs a successful business, over thirty years later. His mother joined him in Johannesburg shortly after his arrival. He often jokes in his impeccable English that he will return to South America as soon as he masters the English language.

Years passed and Norman established himself in South Africa, both financially and socially. He became an activist for the left-wing "Hashomer Hatza'ir" youth movement and quickly rose to the top of its ranks to become one the group's "movers." Religion still was not featured on his agenda. His business flourished and as time passed, the urgency began mounting for the now very eligible young man to find himself a wife. By the early 1980's he had still not met his soul mate, and his friends and relatives upped the pressure, as well as the proposals.

Over the years he returned to his birthplace a couple of times, as did his mother, although never together. In 1984, his mother once again journeyed to Buenos Aires for a short visit. Prior to her departure, she called her son to bid him farewell. In the course of the conversation she mentioned to him how much she would have appreciated having him join her on the trip. "We have both been to your father's grave numerous times," she sighed, "but never have we been there together."

Over the next few days, Norman mulled over his mother's parting words. It had never concerned him that they had not visited the grave together; he never was particularly superstitious. Nevertheless, it bothered him that his mother was disturbed. A week later, he woke up one morning and decided he was going to meet his mother in Argentina. She was still in Buenos Aires and he phoned her and told her that he was on his way. He did, however, caution her not to mention to anyone that he was going to be in town, for fear of being hounded by numerous matchmakers. Not that he was against meeting potential mates; on the contrary, Norman was afraid that he might meet someone suitable and be unable to cement any real relationship into place before he would have to return to Johannesburg. He was to be in Argentina for only five days.

A day later he found himself aboard a South African Airways jet flying high above the deep blue Atlantic. He was excited to be returning once again to his homeland and he was in a holiday frame of mind. Up ahead he noticed two youngsters seated alongside one another. He approached them and introduced himself. Within a few moments they were bantering like old friends, and by the time the plane landed at the Ezeiza International Airport, all had agreed to get together again during the course of their vacations. The fact that the youngsters were not Jewish never troubled Norman.

On his arrival at his hotel, Norman was surprised to see his newfound friends also standing in the lobby. It just so happened that they had all booked into the same hotel, and once again they struck up a friendly conversation. While checking in, the three of them were invited to an evening reception for guests of the hotel.

The threesome settled down, and a short while later were joined by another young group of guests. As the evening wore on, the group broke up and drifted off in groups of twos or threes and Norman noticed one young lady at the far end of the room whom he had never seen before. One of the other guests began to introduce the two of them, when he was called away, and the two were left to strike up a conversation themselves, when Norman asked her name. "Rebecca," came the reply. Somewhat taken aback, he asked for her surname.

Now it was her chance to be astonished.

"Why do you want to know my surname?" she asked indignantly.

Secretly he suspected that she was Jewish, but he could not tell her that.

"Just curious," he replied, somewhat guardedly.

"Actually, it is Kramer," she replied, smiling, "if that makes any difference."

A minute earlier he would have placed money on the chance of there not being a single Jew within a ten-mile radius. Now he was talking to one.

Two hours later, the two were just getting to know each other. He learned that she was working for a recording company and had just received a transfer option to Miami, which she intended to accept. She had also been born in Buenos Aires. He told her all about his move to Africa, his subsequent successes, and of his return to Argentina for the sake of his mother. When they finally got up, both had agreed to meet again the next day. Over the next four days the two met a few more times. Then it was time to say goodbye. No further plans were made; Rebecca was still adamant that she was going to Miami, Norman was firmly committed to Africa.

Over the next few months the two kept in touch with an occasional phone call, although it seemed that nothing more would come from their friendship. Rebecca's imminent departure to Miami would seal that fact, probably forever. Then one day Norman got a call. It was Rebecca, sounding extremely distressed.

"I'm ready to leave for Miami," she told him. "I've got my job, I've got my ticket, my passport, even my bag is packed —"

"And?" he asked, unsure of what she wanted from him.

"They denied me a visa!" she sobbed. Clearly she was just looking for a shoulder to cry on.

Norman's mind was racing. He took a deep breath and tried to steady his tongue.

"Listen carefully, Rebecca," he began. "Don't unpack!"

Rebecca arrived in South Africa a few days later, and two years after that fateful phone call, the two were married. During the two years prior to his marriage Norman discovered that being a Jew meant more than just having a Jewish name, and with some motivation from Rebecca, the two took their first steps along the long but satisfying path of *teshuvah*.

Thanks to a spur-of-the-moment visit to his birthplace for the sake of his mother, with the help of some non-Jewish travelers, and courtesy of an uncharacteristic visa refusal, the two lives of Norman and Rebecca converged and became one.

▪ The Covenant

The evil Turnus Rufus once challenged the great Sage Rabbi Akiva with the following question: "If He [Hashem] wants circumcision, why does the infant not exit his mother's womb already circumcised?"

Replied Rabbi Akiva, "Why does the child not arrive circumcised? Hashem only gave the mitzvos to the Jews to enable them to attach themselves to Him through them" (Tanchuma: Tazria 5).

Said Rabbi Yishmael: "How great is the commandment of circumcision, for thirteen covenants were attached to it explicitly in the verses!" (Tanchuma Lech Lecha 17).

Among those thirteen covenants is a blessing to have children.

Several years had passed since the joyful day of their union. The happiness and serenity that the newly wedded couple so dearly hoped for was marred by the terrible possibility that they would have no children. Norman and Rebecca were both nearing their 40's when they tied the knot. Now they were suddenly faced with the possibility of not being able to build a family. Desperation and depression began knocking at their door. Both husband and wife poured out their hearts in prayer, and discussed their situation with various rabbis in the hope of finding a solution. Then one day, Rebecca was struck by a chilling thought: "Maybe our troubles are all because Norman never had a proper *bris milah*?"

Unlike most Jews, Norman was not circumcised as a baby. His father saw very little value in the "archaic" practices of his own parents and chose not to involve his son in matters he did not believe in. He enrolled the child in a school which had a similar philosophy to his own, and as Norman grew up, he remained unaware of his religious predicament. Then one year Norman was sent away to a holiday camp for children, and although the camp had no religious agenda, it was there that Norman learned about circumcision — and realized that most his peers, even those with little connection to Judaism, had "entered into the covenant". On his arrival back home from the camp, the little 12-year-old cornered his father. "Why haven't I been circumcised like all Jews?" he asked. All his father could do was shrug his shoulders.

A week after returning from the camp, Norman came down with a terrible bout of appendicitis. He was immediately hospitalized and prepped for surgery, and a few hours later the operation was performed. The next morning as the anesthetic wore off and Norman's head began to clear, he saw his father standing alongside his bed. "How are you doing?" he asked. Norman nodded weakly. "Oh, and by the way," his father continued very matter-of-factly, "I had them circumcise you while you were under."

As the years went by, *bris milah* came to mean as little to Norman as it had meant to his father, and not long after the operation, he banished the whole episode to the back of his mind. Life was coming at him too fast to dwell on those types of things. Fortunately, when his religious resurgence commenced shortly before his marriage, he just happened to mention to Rebecca how he had almost not had a *bris*. That was what she was referring to when she mentioned it to him one day as they contemplated their childless existence. Norman was somewhat taken aback by his wife's supposition, but promised to make some inquiries. That night he phoned his good friend Rabbi Michoel Bloch, a *mohel* with thousands of ritual circumcisions to his name.

The *halachah* states that all male Jews are to be circumcised, ideally on the eighth day after their birth. The procedure should be performed by a qualified *mohel*, but in the absence of a *mohel* it can be performed by any other Jew. If, however, a person was circumcised by a non-Jew, or if he was circumcised prior to the eighth day, one is obliged to have a Jew do a simple corrective procedure known as *"hatafas dam bris."*

The phone call lasted no more than a minute:

"Reb Michoel, it's Norman. How are you doing?"

"*Baruch Hashem*, and yourself?"

"Not too bad, although I am a bit concerned."

"Anything I can help with?"

"Well, actually, maybe you can. My wife thinks that we're having trouble having kids because I never had a proper *bris*."

"You what?!"

Norman gave him a brief summary of his situation — about his operation and the non-Jewish surgeon.

"I'm coming right over!" was the last thing he heard before the click on the other end of the line.

"W—w—w—wait a second, I only phoned to discuss it!" he stammered, but the phone had gone dead.

Five minutes later his doorbell rang. As he opened it, the rabbi bustled in, looking very determined. A minute later, it was all over, the procedure being far less traumatic than Norman had expected it to be.

Nine months later to the day, their first child was born.

(Author's note: As I concluded my interview with Norman, Hadassah, their oldest daughter, slipped past the room and disappeared up the stairs. She is now 12 years old, and her brother Levi is 10.)

▪ Burial

Every day has its unique challenge, and every day must be approached with the attitude that it plays a critical role in refining a different element of one's essence. At times it would be nice to be told before the day begins what its particular purpose is, yet this seldom happens. We have to analyze the challenges that get thrown our way during the day, for they are almost always our only clue.

Occasionally, however, one does get a tiny glimpse of the day's challenge before it even starts. A close friend of mine experienced such a glimpse, a glimpse which inspired him to persevere in the face of great odds. The following is a description of this remarkable incident in his own words — and it all began with a serendipitous piece of Talmud.

The Gemara in *Ta'anis* (31a) describes the circumstances surrounding the institution of a fourth blessing in *Bircas HaMazon* by the Sages in Yavneh. Many Jews had died at the time in defense of the city of Betar, and on the day that they were finally allowed to be buried, the Sages saw the need to add an additional prayer of gratitude. An incredible miracle had occurred in that the bodies had not decomposed, despite being exposed to the elements for more than a year. The reason for this blessing was thus twofold: first, that the bodies had not decomposed during that time period, and secondly, that they had now been released for burial. On this particular piece of Gemara, the *Tzlach* (*Berachos* 48b) explains that it was important for those bodies to be buried because the *neshamah* does not go back up to Hashem until the body is suitably interred.

This idea was going around in my head on the evening of January 2. I had learned that particular Gemara earlier in the day and it was still fresh in my mind, but what really made me pay attention to it was the fact that just before I had left for shul that evening, my wife had told me that a distant cousin had passed away, and that the cremation ceremony would be held the next morning. I felt that it was an incredible case of *hashgachah pratis* that I should have learned such a Gemara the very morning that a situation pertaining to the sanctity of a Jewish person's burial would come up in my family.

Immediately after *Ma'ariv*, I called my mother to find out the details of what had transpired. I pointed out that cremation was against Jewish law and that we should do everything in our power to try to prevent it. My mother felt that the attempts would be futile, and did not want to create any rifts in the family. However, I felt we could not leave it at that. I started phoning around to find out who in Johannesburg had experience in dealing with such cases. After several phone calls I discovered that no one really had any constructive suggestions. Furthermore, I was told that attempts to change a cremation to an Orthodox Jewish burial were usually unsuccessful.

After some further deliberation, I decided to phone Rabbi Menachem Raff, the rabbi of my community. He was on vacation at the time and I would not have thought it correct to phone him had it not been for another remarkable instance of *hashgachah pratis*. The day before, we had "bumped" into Rabbi Raff while passing through the town where he was vacationing. I would not normally have phoned Rabbi Raff during the course of his vacation, knowing how important it is for him to rest during these times. However, having seen him the day before, I felt much more comfortable placing the call.

Rabbi Raff's answer was unequivocal: In a situation where there is no one else to act, it is up to you to do whatever you can. The rabbi also gave me some excellent advice on how to approach the situation and how to deal with the family.

I immediately phoned the family. I could not recall ever having spoken to the two children of the deceased. Even though they were both my relatives, probably fourth cousins by my calculations, they were several years older than I and had emigrated from the country some years previously. After offering my condolences I then raised the issue of the cremation. I was speaking to the daughter and I mentioned the Gemara that I had learned that day. Furthermore, I told her that as Jews we have a tradition going back thousands of years that all our ancestors have been buried. I believe these few words made an impression on her, and she said she would call back in a few minutes as she wanted to discuss the issue with her brother.

I anxiously waited for a few minutes before receiving the return phone call. When it came, the answer was that they had considered my proposal, but felt that because it had been their mother's last wish and had been mentioned specifically in her will, they had an obligation to fulfill that wish. I persisted and said that by effecting a burial in the tradition of her forefathers, this in fact would be the highest level of respect that they could show to their mother. She discussed it further with her brother while I held on, and their response was that they felt very strongly that their mother's last wish should be honored. This involved scattering her ashes at the farm where she had lived for over forty years, a property which had subsequently been developed into a residential area in the suburb of Rivonia. I proposed a compromise. I suggested that instead of performing a cremation, perhaps they would consider burying her at the farm, thereby still fulfilling their mother's wish. The response was that if I could arrange it at this late hour, they would be willing to go along with it.

I immediately called up an attorney at a large law firm in Johannesburg. He mentioned that he was not an expert in this particular field of law, but went on to say that the elements of law had changed recently whereby ignorance of the law could in fact be an excuse in certain circumstances. I asked him what the implications would be if we went ahead and buried her without complying with any bylaws or local authority regulations. He felt that in terms of this new change in the law, I would not be liable for prosecution. Seeing this as a situation of literally saving a Jewish *neshamah*, I decided to move ahead on that basis.

The next step was to convince the Johannesburg *Chevrah Kaddisha* to go ahead with the burial on the site in Rivonia. I phoned the head of the *Chevrah Kaddisha*, who said that it was not possible, and that authorization needed to be obtained in advance before they would proceed on such a basis. He further felt that as a prominent Jewish organization, they could not be exposed to any negative publicity which could result from something that was contrary to the law. In the meantime, I was also growing concerned about the fact that the body was lying at the mortuary ready for cremation in the morning. I succeeded in convincing the *Chevrah Kaddisha* to collect the body from the mortuary in order that it would be under their auspices and under the supervision of a Jewish person. Eventually the *Chevrah Kaddisha* arranged to pick up the body at about midnight.

The next morning after *davening,* I received a call from the *Chevrah Kaddisha*, who wanted to know the Hebrew name of the lady who had passed away. I immediately called up her family, who informed me that they did not know this, but that a certain relative of theirs would know the name. In another amazing case of *hashgachah pratis*, it turned out that this relative was a well-known Orthodox Rabbi. I immediately called him up, apprised him of the situation, and asked him to join forces with me in what I felt was a holy mission.

I knew that things were going to get rather hectic as the morning wore on, and we decided to head immediately to the family and then on to the house in Rivonia. On the way down to the house I received a phone call from the head of the *Chevrah Kaddisha* giving me the name of a contact person at the Johannesburg Council who, he said, might be able to help us. I immediately called him up, but after having discussed the matter with him for several minutes, his words were, "The council strongly recommends against performing the burial at the house." We now found ourselves in a very difficult predicament, in that the *Chevrah Kaddisha* was not happy to go ahead with the burial. Neither the rabbi nor myself were comfortable doing something so blatantly against the council's recommendation either. It appeared that we were going to lose our battle against the cremation after all.

During the course of the morning, some of the workers who had been living on the property for many years had begun digging a grave for their beloved boss. Together with the rabbi, I approached the son and presented the situation to him. In another remarkable turn of *siyata d'shemaya*, he came up with the unusual idea of placing the body in the grave that had been dug at Rivonia – then lifting up the coffin and transplanting it to Westpark for a proper Jewish burial. Once formal permission had been obtained from the council, they would then move the body back to the grave site in Rivonia. We all readily agreed that this would be the best solution under the circumstances.

I immediately called up the *Chevrah Kaddisha* and explained the procedure to them. Despite the bizarre nature of the arrangement, they were willing to go along with it for the sake of saving a Jewish *neshamah*. I then asked the *Chevrah Kaddisha* if they could find out whether this lady's parents had been buried at Westpark. I wanted to see if they could find a vacant gravesite nearby. The *Chevrah Kaddisha* phoned back about half an hour later to say that indeed, both her parents were buried at Westpark. Both were buried in a very old section but, incredibly, there was one last remaining gravesite within a few feet of where the parents had been buried together.

From then on, things progressed quite smoothly. The *Chevrah Kaddisha* brought the body from Westpark through to Rivonia where the coffin was laid into the grave but not covered. A few words were said at the gravesite by the family, and many friends and relatives were in attendance. Thereafter, the coffin was lifted up and transported by the *Chevrah Kaddisha* through to Westpark. There, the full burial ceremony took place and Kaddish was said for this lady.

And all because of an unusual Gemara which I had learned the day before.

f the 613 commandments and prohibitions enumerated in the Torah, quite a large number serve as reminders of the events surrounding the Exodus from Egypt. *Tefillin*, Pesach, *mezuzah*, the recitation of *Shema* and dwelling in a *succah* are but a few of these, whose function is to ensure that we remember what occurred to our ancestors when they were freed from their bondage.

The importance of remembering this event over and above other great historical occurrences is that it serves to reinforce four fundamentals elements of our belief. Not only did the Creator verify His existence, but He also demonstrated that He is keenly aware of the events transpiring on earth, and confirmed that He will intervene on behalf of an individual or group of people. The fact that these unnatural events were predicted by Moshe *Rabbeinu* confirms the validity of the concept of prophecy, that the Creator does communicate with human beings, and reveals hidden matters to His servants the prophets.

Considering that Hashem will not perform such miracles for the benefit of every agnostic, skeptic, or denier who wishes to have his doubts resolved, He saw it necessary to ensure that the message of the events in Egypt be safely entrusted from generation to generation. Consequently, He instructed us to make commemorations and observances which would perpetuate the wonders which the generation of the Exodus witnessed, to be passed on to their children and from them to their children as an affirmation for all generations of these fundamental principles.

And from the great, overt miracles, a person will come to accept and be sensitive to the smaller, more hidden ones. For a person does not have a share in the Torah of Moshe Rabbeinu unless he believes that all of our matters and experiences are all miracles, with no connection whatsoever to nature or "the way of the world" (Ramban).

■ Accurate Scales

When the Torah describes to us the events leading up to the sale of Yosef to the Ishmaelite caravan and his being taken down to Egypt, it describes how the Ishmaelites were transporting "spices, balsam, and lotus, on their way to bring them down to Egypt." The Ishmaelite caravans at the time were known to have carried only tar and oil, commodities which emit foul-smelling fumes, which would certainly have made the journey most uncomfortable for the righteous Yosef (Rashi).

Rav Chaim Shmulevitz, zt"l, explained that although the Divine master plan necessitated Yosef's being sold into slavery – for the sake of his own destiny and the destiny of the entire Jewish people – it was not necessary for Yosef to suffer unduly on the way down. Hashem wanted Yosef in Egypt, but He made sure that on his journey Yosef did not experience even one iota of discomfort more than was required.

We must remember that even the minutest details in our lives are measured out precisely according to our needs. Every microgram of pain, milliliter of joy, moment of discomfort, or cent of loss is measured on the most accurate of scales and distributed accordingly.

The following story captures this idea perfectly.

For those eager to strike up warm relationships with the great *Roshei Yeshivah* of Eretz Yisrael, South Africa would not be the first place to look for them. Jerusalem, Bnei Brak, New York, or even London perhaps, but South Africa? Despite this common misconception. it is in this distant place that numerous laymen have had the unique opportunity of spending quality time with *gedolim*. In years gone by, South Africa has been graced by visits of the Ponevizher Rav, HaRav Yosef Shlomo Kahaneman, *zt"l*, Rav Simcha Wasserman, *zt"l*, and, *yibadel l'chaim*, HaRav Yissachar Meir among numerous other illustrious guests. These Torah giants journey southwards to gather support for their vital institutions, to deliver inspiration and encouragement to sagging communities, or simply to visit friends and relatives residing in this far-flung African land.

One of these perennial visitors once related the following story to me:

It is common practice among visiting rabbis to hire a driver, often an unemployed member of the community, to take them around their community. With this "chauffeur" at his disposal, the rabbi can be certain that he will get to see all the people on his itinerary within the shortest amount of time possible.

One year, after a busy week in Johannesburg, this particular rabbi informed his driver that he would no longer require his services, since someone had offered to chauffeur him for the rest of his stay. It was a Thursday night. To the rabbi's surprise, however, the driver pleaded to be allowed to work the following day, even free of charge. He explained to the rabbi that he would end up spending the entire Friday cooped up in his apartment getting depressed, and would rather spend it in the rabbi's company. The rabbi acceded to his request and they agreed to settle their financial business only after the following day's travels, even though the man did not want payment for the day. The driver dropped the rabbi at his place of residence and arranged to return the following morning to pick him up.

Not two hours later, the rabbi received a phone call. It was the driver. While parking his vehicle outside his apartment block, he had been held up by a group of armed men. Not satisfied with only taking his car, they had also emptied his pockets of any valuables, removed his watch from his arm, and pilfered his mobile telephone. The driver was calling to let the rabbi know that he would not be available to transport him the next day, as he no longer had a car at his disposal.

The rabbi made a silent observation: For whatever reason, it had been decided Above that this hapless driver would today lose his car, his watch, his telephone, and a certain amount of money. What had also been decided Above, however, was that he should not lose his "chauffeur" pay.

He tied this observation to a verse in *Tehillim* (19:10): "The judgments of Hashem are true, individually righteous." Rabbi Eliyahu Dessler, in his classic work *Michtav Me'Eliyahu*, explains this verse to mean that before any judgment is carried out in the world, Hashem assesses its potential effect on each and every person down to the finest detail.

▪ Cholent

The word "cholent," much like the word "chutzpah," has managed to find its way into the English language. Defining it appropriately, however, is quite another story. Some would find themselves using the word "stew" in their description, a word which is wholly inadequate, as it fails to do justice to the unique flavors and special quality of this exclusively Jewish dish. There are very few people in the world who would consider cooking a large pot of meat, beans, potatoes, and a motley assortment of other ingredients for close to twenty-four hours, to be eaten at lunchtime. Then again, few people are Jewish.

There is a perception that the custom of preparing cholent is simply a practical consideration, resulting from the fact that it is not permissible to prepare hot dishes on the Shabbos day, and one must therefore prepare them the day before. The custom of eating cholent is actually firmly rooted in tradition, and for good reason. Many years ago there were groups of

*Jews who splintered away from mainstream Judaism and had
the temerity to suggest that the written Torah was to be taken at
face value, without the explanation provided by the Oral
Torah. Thus when they read the verse, "You shall not light a fire
in all your habitations on the Shabbos day," they took it literally
and banned any forms of fire from their homes on the
Shabbos, including those fires lit prior to the onset of Shabbos.
Thus they spent a miserable Shabbos each week shivering in
the dark and eating cold foods. To their mistaken interpretation,
it became customary to prepare a hot meal for the Shabbos
day, and thus the concept of cholent came into being.*

*A close relative of mine recently explained to me that
there are, however, occasions when the rules of this custom
have to be slightly bent, as he and his wife experienced not
too long ago...*

The Friday-night service had just drawn to a close, and Hillel
was preparing to set out homeward where his young wife
waited. Only recently married, he was certain that she had an ap-
petizing meal awaiting his return, and he felt his stomach rumble
slightly at the thought. A tap on his elbow brought him quickly
out of his reverie. It was Yaakov Garb, his friend's son, with a
message from his mother.

"My mother asked me to tell you that we will be starting lunch
tomorrow at about 12:30, if that is okay with you."

Hillel hesitated, a look of confusion showing briefly on his face,
before he succeeded in stifling it with a smile. "That is perfect," he
said, and then added somewhat untruthfully, "We've been looking forward to it the whole week."

The truth was that Hillel knew nothing of such arrangements,
and he was certain that his wife was also blissfully unaware. He
had seen his wife preparing a cholent on *erev* Shabbos, so she had
obviously forgotten about the invitation, if she had even known
about it in the first place.

As Hillel walked up the hill toward his house, he pondered how best to break the news to his wife. By the time he arrived at his front door, he had decided that the best way to deal with the oversight was with a bit of humor. So when Yael came out to greet him, he jokingly exclaimed, "How about having some cholent for dinner?" When he explained to her what he meant, relating the message he had received in shul, she slapped her forehead dramatically. "Of course! How could I have forgotten?"

The incident was quickly put aside as their appetites soon reminded them of the more immediate Shabbos meal. After *Kiddush* wine and challah, the fish course only served to whet their appetites, and when it came time for the meat course, they found themselves licking their lips eagerly. Yael disappeared into the kitchen, and a minute later Hillel heard her summoning him. "Come look at this," she called in a strange voice. Hillel found her standing in the kitchen, peering cautiously at a large brisket sitting in a roasting pan on the counter. She pointed gingerly at the meat, and Hillel moved closer. Something was wrong with the meat; it seemed to be spoiled.

Yael turned to Hillel and said, "What now?"

Without skipping a beat, Hillel replied triumphantly, "Let's hit that cholent of yours, and hooray to the Garbs!"

▪ Fishy Find

After our forefather Avraham made the heartbreaking decision of sending away his maidservant Hagar and her son Yishmael for the sake of Yitzchak's upbringing, Hagar found herself in the desert with no water to slake her feverish son's thirst. The verse then says, "And Hashem opened up her eyes and she beheld a well of water, and she went and she filled up the flask, and she gave the boy to drink" (Bereishis 21:19).

On this verse the Midrash explains: "Rabbi Binyamin says, Everyone is in the category of the blind, until Hashem lights up their eyes" (Midrash Rabbah 53:14).

This aphorism is demonstrated clearly by the following personal experience, a story which shows how even the smallest financial loss or gain is calculated into the Divine master plan.

It was a difficult invitation to turn down. A group of friends were traveling down to the northern coast of Zululand on a three-day scuba-diving expedition, and had offered me the opportunity of tagging along. Despite my nonexistent diving experience, I readily signed up, not with the intention of gaining that experience but rather with the objective of getting a break from my teaching schedule and perhaps splashing around in the shallow water with a mask and snorkel. Our party consisted of a couple of businessmen, as well as a group of young university students, except for one youth who had just completed high school. Saul was in limbo at the time, debating whether to immediately pursue a career, or to first spend some time in a yeshivah.

Our destination was Sodwana Bay, by far the most popular diving spot in Southern Africa, and one of the most pristine and undamaged underwater sanctuaries in the world. The warm Mozambique current flows down the Kwazulu-Natal coast, allowing the world's southernmost tropical reefs to flourish. Up to 1200 species of fish have been identified in and around Sodwana Bay. I was excited to be going to such a unique and pure part of the country.

The reefs at Sodwana run parallel to the shore and are named for their distance from Jesser Point, the site from which the diving boats launch. The unimaginative names of these reefs – Quarter Mile, Two Mile, Five Mile, Seven Mile, and Nine Mile – belie the beauty and sheer diversity of the marine life which can be observed in the vicinity of these popular diving spots.

Despite a considerable amount of pressure from my fellow travelers, and a strong pull to experience these underwater marvels, I was resolute in my decision to limit my marine exposure to the shallow water around the bay. As they headed out to the boat on the first day, toting large oxygen cylinders and clad in sinister black wetsuits, I armed myself with snorkel, mask, and flippers and waded into the bay.

It is a dizzyingly marvelous experience the first time one submerges one's mask below the surface — a totally unique experience akin to the first time one balances on a bike or flies in an airplane. A moment earlier you were waddling around like an inexperienced duck thanks to your flippers, breathing strangely through an incongruous tube called a snorkel, all the while trying to see where you were going through a mask pressing against your nose. Ahead of you the surface of the water stretches to the horizon – restless, lifeless, and monotonously blue.

As your mask breaks the surface, it is as if you have been teleported into a different world, a world functioning in a different dimension. The first thing that strikes you is the color. A small angelfish wanders past, outrageously decorated in yellow and blue stripes, followed by a gaudily outfitted cleaner wrasse. Schools of color flit past your masked eyes, like the miniature canvases of some joyous and highly eccentric painter. As you slowly begin to digest the rainbow of colors, you are suddenly struck by the sounds, a sensory experience which most people assume is not found below the surface. The coral crackles as the tiny organisms that constitute it shift and expand, the waves sizzle overhead and then tinkle as they break, while the fish swish softly as they flit curiously around the strange creature which has suddenly appeared in their midst. It is a thoroughly captivating experience.

Later in the day, I was joined by Saul and his brother Clive who, having returned from the deep-sea excursion on Quarter Mile reef, were interested in seeing what the shallow waters had to offer. We paddled around aimlessly for a while, admiring the gaily colored creatures and their curious habits. As I swam, I noticed a bright blue spot on the sandy bottom which, after careful observation, turned out to be the distinctive marking on the back of a blue-spotted stingray. I excitedly summoned my colleagues, who hastily joined me to study the unusual creature. We remained suspended in the clear water above the ray for a considerable amount of time, during which Saul removed his flippers at some point. When we arrived at the shore a short while later he suddenly realized that he was missing one of his flippers. He was understandably upset, for the flipper had been a state-of-the-art model and had cost him a considerable sum of money.

We spent the next half-hour scouring the shallow waters for the missing flipper. After experimenting with the remaining one, we determined that the missing appendage would have sunk immediately, and subsequently we focused our search bottomward. After a while, we gave up the search, having found the very same ray which we had been studying at the time of the loss, but not the errant flipper. Saul resigned himself to the loss, and borrowed another pair for the rest of the trip.

Two months after our return to Johannesburg, Saul decided to spend a few months in yeshivah to gain some Torah experience before facing the "real" world. On the day that he signed up, he received a phone call. It was the diving instructor who had led their dives. He had found Saul's flipper. On Nine Mile reef.

Purely by "chance," the very man who had led their dives had spotted the missing piece of equipment, *nine miles* up the coast from the point where Saul had lost it! The flipper was still marked with Saul's initials. He is adamant that its extraordinary discovery was directly linked to his decision to further his Torah studies.

Nine miles up the coast, two months later, and on the day he started yeshivah.

▪ Accidents

In Psalm 92, King David writes, "How great are Your deeds, Hashem; exceedingly profound are Your thoughts. A boor cannot know, and a fool cannot understand this." Rabbi Ezriel Tauber once explained that when it comes to rejecting the perfection of the world and the Torah, there are two categories of people: the fools and the boors. To the boor who is uneducated and insensitive to the finer details of the universe, everything is incomprehensible. He does not pretend to understand, and maintains that nothing makes sense and that there is little coordination in the world, chas v'shalom. There is, however, a worse category: the man who picks out one tiny detail and proclaims, "It is this that does not make sense."

The follies of the two categories can be summed up by the following parable: Two men are granted an exclusive opportunity to tour the state-of-the-art mission-control center at NASA. The first enters the room and is overwhelmed by the astounding array of screens, dials, buttons, knobs, and machinery. After a few moments of contemplation, he resigns himself to the fact that he cannot understand a single part of its workings. His friend follows along close behind him, and after a minute of casual study, turns to one of the scientists standing there and asks the following question: "Why does this little button over here have an arrow on it pointing to the side? Surely if you are sending spacecrafts up and down it should have an arrow indicating that."

Undoubtedly, the second man is the fool, for he implies that everything is obvious to him, and he is only troubled by one small question.

We must not make the mistakes of the two NASA visitors. We must remember that there is an infinitely powerful Designer coordinating this existence and that indeed His thoughts are "exceedingly profound." The following incident occurred to an uncle of mine.

For a new immigrant, Jeff Miller had done well for himself. Only five years after touching down on Australian soil, he and his family were integrating well into their new surroundings and were already contributing significantly to the Sydney Jewish community. The steel-processing plant Jeff had bought from the brink of bankruptcy was back in the black, and expansion and growth were the major goals on his horizon, a challenge which he relished greatly. The Millers' successful transition had been greatly influenced by a large dollop of South African optimism and energy which they had packed together with their luggage, and there was little on the horizon to muffle those feelings.

It was a Tuesday morning and Jeff was on one of his regular reconnaissance rambles through his warehouse building, checking on the productivity of his staff. It has been said that a good businessman can assess the bottom line of his organization without even glancing at a single piece of paper, for the tune being played by his work force and their tools often tells more of the story than the most detailed balance sheets. As he walked down the aisles between the large rolls of stainless steel, many standing taller than his own six feet, Jeff swung his arms casually at his sides, taking in the sights and sounds of his bustling concern. Suddenly, he felt his hand bump against something on his side, and a burning pain seared up his right arm. He looked down to see blood gushing from two fingers on the inside of his right hand.

Instinctively he clenched his hand closed and dashed for the main office. There, he wrapped a bandage around the wounded fingers, clenched his hand closed once again, and ran to find someone to take him to the hospital. This one, he knew, was serious.

As they raced toward the hospital, his mind dissected the duration of that fateful second, trying to understand how from one moment to the next everything had turned upside down. What he deducted was that purely by chance, the end of one of the steel rolls standing alongside the aisle had been facing toward him as he walked by. His swinging hand just happened to collide with the razor-sharp end of the roll, which cut deeply into his little and ring fingers.

Half an hour later, they arrived at the emergency room of a clinic in downtown Sydney. There, Jeff unclenched the hand for the first time since applying the bandage, and the doctor gingerly removed the dressing. A brief examination by the doctor quickly ascertained that surgery was needed, and he bandaged the hand once again and scurried off to summon a surgeon. The tendons in both fingers were severed together with the nerves, and only thanks to the wonders of microsurgery would he ever have use of his fingers again. A further half-hour passed before Jeff was wheeled into the operating room. The last thing he was conscious of was the anesthetist's masked face peering down at him. Then everything went black.

Five hours later, the world swam past his eyes again. This time it was the concerned face of the surgeon peering down at him, although the man appeared to be floating in some sort of bizarre liquid. Jeff desperately wanted to reach up and stabilize the poor fellow, but his arms felt pinned to his sides as if he was being sat upon by an overweight elephant. Through the anesthetic-induced haze he began catching snippets of what sounded vaguely like English, and which appeared to be emanating from somewhere below the floating doctor's chin. "Complicated … three-and-a-half hours … very delicate … microsuturing … ." The words floated through the vacuum which now existed within his skull, without finding anything upon which to rest. "Lucky … removed … laboratory … tumor … ." Jeff suddenly sat bolt upright, or at least his brain ordered his body to do so with little success. The spinning room came to a dizzying halt. He had heard the last word which the doctor had uttered, and abruptly he was wide awake. The doctor must have moved to the next bed, he reassured himself, and was probably addressing a different patient. When he opened his eyes again, however, the doctor was still peering down at him. "Mr. Miller," the face said, "can you hear me?"

Gradually, the story filtered into his chemically addled head. After opening up the damaged ring finger to reconnect the tendons and nerves, the surgeon had discovered an inch-long growth along the length of the tendon. During the three-hour operation, he had not only reconnected the severed nerves and tendons but had also painstakingly removed the tumor.

A short while later, the laboratory results came through, indicating that the growth was noncancerous. Nevertheless, the surgeon was quick to point out that had the tumor gone undetected for another few months, it could quite easily have permanently damaged the nerves and tendons in the finger. The doctor examined the rest of Jeff's fingers and found them all free of any such growths.

Were it not for the "accidental" injury inflicted on the very finger which contained the tumor, Jeff might not have had the use of his finger for the remainder of his life.

▪ Lights Out

When Moshe was on Har Sinai praying for G-d's mercy after the disaster of the Golden Calf, at one point he asked Hashem to demonstrate to him His glory. The response of Hashem was cryptic: "…you will see My back, but My face may not be seen." My teacher, Rav Aharon Pfeuffer, z"tl, once presented an interpretation of Chazal on this difficult verse. He explained that, prior to an event, one can never understand what the meaning of the event is, or why Hashem will perform it. Similarly, during an event one is unable to comprehend Hashem's reasoning and motivations. However, at times, a great person is able to look back at an event and understand Hashem's workings in the world. This, he said, was the meaning of "…you will see My back, but My face may not be seen."

The following is a story which I witnessed in person, yet which I could only appreciate fully once I had gotten all the background information from the person to whom it happened. What makes this story so beautiful is the exquisite coordination of a few events running parallel in time. It is a story which truly awakens us to the amazing timing which affects each and every one of our lives.

It was Tuesday afternoon, the day before Pesach, and Ian detected a jovial atmosphere in his office as he wended his way through the corridors of the large import agency that he owned in Johannesburg. The cause of the high spirits was fairly obvious, for although most of his staff members were gentiles or nonobservant Jews, they were all given the days of the Pesach festival as paid leave, and it was clear to Ian that they were already relishing the prospect. After perusing the productivity and positivism of his own staff, Ian rambled onwards through the wing of his building occupied by his Israeli tenant. He was surprised to note a distinctly down-beat and brooding atmosphere among the people working there. Somewhat miffed by the stark contrast, he turned to his tenant's secretary and asked her whether she was looking forward to her break. The confused look on her face was all it took to explain the situation to Ian. Clearly, his tenant was not planning to shut down his operation for *Yom Tov*.

In a fit of zealousness, Ian knocked on his tenant's office door and barged in when the man beckoned. "Avi, what is going on here?" Ian asked. In the ensuing animated and heated debate, Ian tried valiantly to impress upon his tenant the importance of respecting the sanctity of the festival, while Avi argued equally vigorously that he could not afford to close shop and lose so many working days. When it became obvious to Ian that Avi was not going to close, he handed him an ultimatum. "If you are going to work here on *Yom Tov*," he told Avi firmly, "the lights are to be turned off, so that no one should think that I have sanctioned what is going on here." With that he turned on his heel and left the office.

The next day as Ian rushed homeward to prepare for *Yom Tov*, his cell phone rang. With one hand on the steering wheel Ian took the call, and was surprised to hear the voice of his tenant on the line. "You were right, Ian," said Avi. "It's probably better if I don't open up on *Yom Tov*. I just phoned to let you know that no work will take place in your building tomorrow." Ian entered *Yom Tov* with a warm glow in his heart, a result of the disaster which he felt he had averted.

On the afternoon of the second day of *Yom Tov*, Ian retired after lunch for a short nap to work off the effects of two late nights and eight glasses of red wine. Needless to say, he underestimated his tiredness, and woke up with a start at 5:40 in the evening. He lurched out of bed and began throwing on his clothes, for he knew all too well that his regular *minyan* at the Yeshivah Maharsha *beis midrash* would not wait for him. The *minyan* started at 5:45 and the walk took approximately twelve minutes. At 5:44 Ian scuttled out his front door. Glancing at his watch every few seconds, he set out up the hill toward Maharsha.

Like almost every other Jew in the world, Ian is accustomed to walk past two other shuls on his way to Maharsha. This phenomenon of having a shul to "not *daven* at" can only be ascribed to the well-known idea of "*sechar pesi'os,*" that a person's reward is greatly increased for each step he takes to arrive at a *mitzvah.* Thus as Ian made his way up the hill on that Pesach afternoon, he fought the huge temptation of simply dropping in to the Ohr Same'ach *beis midrash* to catch a *Minchah minyan.* As he was about to pass by the shul, a friend of his called from the gate. "Ian, come inside, you're going to miss *Minchah* if you try to get to your own shul." For a moment Ian faltered, but then he stepped impulsively into the inviting interior of the shul. He stood for a moment watching the preparations for the prayers going on around him. Suddenly, he recalled that at his own *beis midrash,* one of the young yeshivah students was scheduled to address the community after *Minchah.* Ian also remembered that his own son would also be speaking there in a few days. A pang of guilt stabbed him. How could he miss someone else's son's moment of glory and then expect others to attend when his own son spoke? He strode purposefully out of the shul and once again pointed his steps in the direction of Maharsha, determined not to let anything get in his way.

A few blocks later, he neared the second shul he was to pass on his route. It was 5:51 and in the distance he could make out a fellow congregant of Maharsha who waved to him and shouted, "You're gonna be late if you go to Maharsha. They'll be finished *davening* by the time you get there," indicating that they should both stop and pray at the shul. Ian, however, had his mind set and not much would get in his way now.

While Ian raced through the streets of Glenhazel, something unusual was going on at Maharsha. Known for its punctiliousness and attention to detail, it has been said in jest that the Swiss themselves could set their watches by the clocks at Maharsha, yet on that Pesach afternoon, the impossible had happened. One of the non-Jewish staff members had turned off the main lights in the shul, leaving the room cloaked in late-afternoon gloom. None of the staff were anywhere to be found and shortly before 5:45, the designated time for *Minchah*, a frantic search began to find a non-Jew to rectify the problem. (It is permitted in very specific circumstances to use a non-Jew to perform activities forbidden on Shabbos or Festivals, and this story should not be used as a precedent). With the *gabbai* looking anxiously at his watch, the shul property was scoured for a single gentile, but to no avail. As predicted by Murphy in his famous laws of probability, the normally busy streets outside the shul were suddenly bereft of any non-Jewish passersby.

After a few minutes of frantic searching, someone found a security guard standing in a nearby street. When they tried to explain to him the situation, he would not budge, for he was going off shift at that moment and did not want to miss his ride home. With no other choice, the *gabbai* sent his son to bring the maid from their house. At 5:54, the wizened old woman finally creaked into the shul and rekindled the lights.

At 5:55, Ian puffed up to his place in the shul to hear the *chazan* chanting the opening line of *Minchah*.

He had caught his *minyan*.

As he reached his place, Ian beheld a remarkable sight, for there in the seat adjacent to his stood his tenant Avi, dressed in *Yom Tov* finery. "I walked halfway across town to wish you a *Good Yom Tov*," said the man who a day earlier was prepared to desecrate the festival for a few extra bucks. Then with a smile he added: "I was worried for a moment that you would not make it."

And Ian just smiled knowingly.

Of all the wondrous miracles which the Israelites experienced as they journeyed triumphantly out of Egypt, it was only the miracle of the manna which they were instructed to capture for future generations. A single helping of the heavenly bread was placed in a jar to be preserved for all future offspring to see, as a tangible reminder: "This is the way our forefathers were sustained during the forty years they traveled in the barren desert." There is a vital lesson which can be gleaned from the miracle of the manna, a lesson which Hashem wanted preserved for every generation, and one which is relevant to this very day.

The Torah records a most unusual phenomenon which occurred when the Israelites went out to gather the manna. Every day, a member of each household, the "breadwinner," would travel to the edges of the camp to gather what he assumed to be sufficient manna for himself and his dependents. He would then lug his bounty back to his tent where his eager family waited. On his arrival back home, the tired breadwinner would quickly measure his takings to ascertain how much he had indeed brought home. A great surprise awaited these men, for no matter how much they gathered on each given day, the calculations always showed there to be exactly enough for the household, one *omer* per person!

What we can learn from the events surrounding the manna is that, even after gathering what one believes to be sufficient for his household, what a man "brings home" is completely in the Hands of Hashem.

▪ Nothing But a Sample

The Talmud states that the exact measure of a man's livelihood is allotted to him at Rosh Hashanah, the beginning of the Jewish Year. Our Sages have told us that every person is obliged nevertheless to perform the normal exertion accepted in society to earn his allocation.

Elsewhere, the Talmud observes that earning a livelihood is "as difficult as the splitting of the Sea of Reeds." When the Jewish nation arrived at the sea, they had run out of options. The Midrash relates how they were completely trapped, with the sea to the one side, wild animals on another, and the Egyptian army bearing down on them from behind. The hallmark of that experience was that the salvation came from the most unexpected quarter. Had they considered their options at the time, no one would have imagined in which direction their rescue lay. Earning a livelihood is much the same, for all too often, things look bleak and beyond rescue. The message at the sea was never to give up, for salvation can come from the most unexpected quarter.

This was a lesson brought home to a prominent member of the Johannesburg community a few years ago. This is the story he told me.

In the dog-eat-dog world of modern-day business, qualifications are everything. Never before has the ability to flash your gilt-edged card, to wave your cum laude credentials been as important as it is today. In days of yore, knights in shining armor tallied their conquests and victories with small notches on the hilt of their swords. Today, dynamic executives measure their success by the number of acronyms and initials that march after their name on the brass plate decorating their office doors. A man will sacrifice three years of his life on the altar of higher education, all so that three simple letters can be appended to his autograph.

Had someone told the poor fellow's mother how important those letters would be one day, she could have stuck it on the birth certificate thirty years earlier and saved him a lot of trouble.

There is, however, one credential, one qualification, which no learning institution in the world can issue. It is a title recognized internationally and one which inspires respect and almost inevitably ensures business ingenuity. The MsK, or Master of *Sechel* and *Kop*, is a distinction awarded to a privileged few, and which has gained tremendous acclaim over the last few centuries worldwide. It has become synonymous with superb business acumen and an uncanny knack for making the right move at the right time. Many simply refer to it as a *"Yiddishe kop."*

It was this very qualification which was causing Alan Wallensky so much grief. His business, a robust and dynamic clothing company, was doing nicely. Turnover was high, profit margins even higher (although obviously not more than the proverbial "10 percent" referred to by all MsKs), even the taxman was being kept at bay. Yet something told him that he needed to be aware that his market share, despite being an ample slice of the pie, would not stay that way. Deep down he understood that the company needed to grow, and that even a stable and profitable company can stagnate and quickly lose its market dominance. He perceived that the only way to expand his concern was to go national, to market his products through the powerful and pervasive chain stores with branches in all the main centers. An "in" with one of these retailing giants would mean unprecedented growth for his operation. What troubled him was how to get that "in."

Alan kept his ear to the ground, and his other ear he kept to the telephone and his network of friends in the wholesale game. When a belated tip-off finally slithered through the telephone wires, it didn't exactly have him dancing on his desk. Southfords, a huge, very exclusive retailing chain, was looking for a supplier of silk ties, a product which Alan happened to promote. What disheartened him was that he knew his neckties would not meet Southfords' high standards of quality. The chain was infamous for its overly particular and meticulous supplier-selection process. Fortunately, some gentle prodding from the friend who gave him the lead eventually prevailed, and Alan landed an appointment to meet the chief buyer for Southfords anyway, at their head office in Cape Town. So great were his misgivings and apprehension about the meeting, however, that he actually booked appointments with a few other chain stores based in Cape Town to justify the trip in his own mind. Perhaps, he rationalized, his break would come from an unexpected source.

On the day of the big meeting, Alan had his secretary carefully pack his samples into a carrying case. In his mind, he reviewed over and over what he was going to tell the buyer, how he was even going to justify taking up the man's time. When the hour to head for the airport arrived, a wave of apprehension clenched his gut. For a moment he considered locking himself in his office and feigning illness, but fortunately prudence prevailed over apprehension.

As he rushed out of his office, his co-director intercepted him in the corridor. He held out a cellophane-wrapped package.

"Take this with you," he said. "It's just arrived from the manufacturer. Show it to Trendz while you're down there; you never know what they might be looking for." Trendz was one of the other chain stores where Alan had booked an appointment.

Alan recognized the package to be a new line of socks they had been waiting for, but knew instantly that Trendz would not even look at them. The socks were far too pricey for the Trendz customer base. Too harried to explain the finer details to his co-director, Alan stuffed the sample into his bag and bustled out the door.

The butterflies which had begun to flit gently in his stomach in Johannesburg seemed to have transformed into vast squadrons of bats by the time Alan's plane touched down in Cape Town. A small nagging voice kept reminding him that just one short phone call could put him out of his misery. A two-minute conversation and the doomed meeting could be canceled. It was only through an extreme feat of self-control that he managed to stay away from the phone and make his way into a waiting cab.

As he entered the main offices of Southfords, Alan silently rehearsed his presentation. He tried to picture an eager, receptive response on the part of the Southfords executives, but, unfortunately, his actual meeting was not so positive. Alan met with the head buyer of Southfords, together with the merchandising director of the chain. They were in the buyer's large office overlooking the beautiful city of Cape Town. With a flourish, Alan produced from his bag the product he had brought to show them and studied their faces for a reaction. As was expected, the men were not hugely excited by Alan's submission.

The meeting lasted barely three minutes, by which time Alan was ready to beat a hasty retreat. The buyer and merchandising director circumnavigated the desk to see him out, while Alan attempted to replace the rejected sample into the bag as inconspicuously as possible. His shaking hands opened the zipper just a bit too far and a small cellophane package fell out of the side. Before he had a chance to stuff it back into the case, the eyes of the buyer lit up.

"What's that?" he exclaimed.

"Um — well — in fact it's one of our sock lines," Alan mumbled, unsure how to interpret the buyer's sudden interest in his goods.

"May I see it?" the man inquired eagerly. "We happen to be looking for just that type of sock at the moment."

The rest of the meeting swirled around him like a blizzard. Minutes later, the man grasped Alan's trembling hand in his own and shook it vigorously. What had begun so poorly had turned completely around and Alan found that he had been nominated as a prestigious supplier of the Southfords' chain. On the spot, the buyer placed an order for all the available stock of the socks, a very substantial order in and of itself.

The elevator was barely big enough to contain the giant grin plastered across Alan's face as he made his way out of the Southfords' building. It would nevertheless take a few hours before the bizarre nature of his windfall finally sank in. In the meantime, his day still had a few more cards to play before it would be considered finshed.

Despite his excitement, Alan still had his other appointments to keep, and from Southfords he went directly to the Trendz head office. There he was met by the director of marketing, one of the most influential men in the company, and a very intimidating figure at that. They greeted and introduced themselves. On hearing Alan's surname, the man's face lit up.

"Are you by any chance related to Hymie Wallensky?" the director inquired.

"If you call a father a relative," replied Alan, "then indeed I am."

The director's demeanor immediately softened. "I worked for your father many years ago, decades ago in fact. Your father was a real gentleman and I owe him a debt of gratitude for what he did for me in those early days.

"Come with me," he said. "Let's see what we can do for you today."

Alan followed the man along the corridor. Presently, they came to an office, that of the head buyer for the chain. The director entered and ushered Alan in after him. He introduced Alan to the buyer, describing to her how indebted he was to the man's father. "Hear him out," he said as he exited the room.

At the buyer's request, Alan spread out all his samples on the desk for her to examine closely. After a few minutes of careful study of the samples, he could see that she was somewhat uncertain what to do. He knew he needed something more, just one small trump card to push the deal over the edge.

Another minute passed and then she asked: "Who else do you supply?"

It was obvious that she was trying to gauge the quality of his operation by his clientele. Alan listed a few of his clients and almost as an afterthought he added: "Oh, we also just signed with Southfords this morning; the first order should be delivered by the end of the week."

The buyer's eyebrows shot up for a fraction of a second, but it was all Alan needed to know that the deal was in the bag. They negotiated for a few more minutes and concluded the business with a large order.

In the course of one tumultuous day, Alan had signed two huge clients, both through amazing serendipity. Ten years down the line both chains are still loyal customers and their patronage has helped Alan develop his company into a major role-player in the industry, and a highly successful concern.

▪ Fruitful Endeavor

With reference to the construction of the Menorah, the candelabra of the Tabernacle, our Sages teach us that Moshe was unable to execute its complex design, and therefore Hashem instructed him to cast the ingot into the fire where it would form on its own. Thus, Moshe did not make the Menorah in the strictest sense of the word, but rather the Menorah was made on his behalf.

However, in another place our Sages tell us that Moshe struggled to understand the detailed construction of the Menorah and he could only comprehend the design after Hashem showed him a fiery image of how it was supposed to look. From this verse and its traditional interpretation, it would seem that Moshe did indeed make the Menorah after being shown how to go about it. The Sfas Emes resolves this difficulty with the following explanation:

If a person desires, wholeheartedly, to complete a mitzvah, *but is held back by limited resources or abilities, Hashem completes the task on his behalf. Thus Moshe, who did not have the wherewithal to sculpt the Menorah, had just to cast the gold into the fire and it was formed on its own. It is imperative, however, for a person to understand exactly what is expected of him, and to aspire wholeheartedly to that target, for only then will Divine assistance manifest itself. Moshe needed to be completely aware of how the finished Menorah should look, so that he could fervently aspire to execute his task, and in that*

*way ensure that Hashem would carry it through to
its completion.*

So it is with any mitzvah *incumbent on anyone, for it is
obvious that a person does not have the wherewithal and
resources to perform Hashem's will (in its entirety). Only as
a result of the person's desire (to execute his duty) is it
completed on its own* (Sfas Emes).

*The following story was told to me by Rabbi Menachem
Raff and is about someone who desperately wanted to fulfill
hakaras hatov — expressing one's gratitude— until he
indeed "achieved" the desired result.*

Most financial experts would be hard pressed to single out
the one most-lucrative investment opportunity available.
Futures, options, derivatives, and mining exploration all rank
high, although any savvy moneyman would concede that when
investing in the likes of these, for every cent potentially pocketed,
there are about ten waiting to be lost. There is, however, one commodity which manages to sneak past the horn-rims of even the
most hawkeyed Wall Streeter, a stock which in its first week offers
dividends so fantastically high that its bearers are even prepared
to overlook the fact that seven days after the stock is issued, it
cheapens to almost a thousandth of its initial value. It is an investment made by almost every well-informed Jew, but only once
a year, and what makes this commodity so unusual is that it takes
the form of a humble citrus fruit — also known as an *esrog.*

By the third week of mulling over his quandary, Harold
Grossberg had all but given up ever finding a solution. The order
had been a significant one, both because of its size and timing,
and his appreciation toward the thoughtful fellow congregant
who had placed it ran deep. What could he do for his insightful
benefactor who had helped him get his business onto its feet, that
would be both meaningful and significant? By the second day of
Succos the problem weighed heavily on his shoulders as he plod-
ded toward shul for the morning prayers.

As he walked, he noticed ahead of him a fellow Jew crossing the road carrying his *lulav* and *esrog*, also headed for one of the many nearby shuls. With an inward groan Harold realized that he had forgotten his own set of *Arbaah Minim* at home, and reluctantly he redirected his steps homewards to correct his error. Having collected what he needed, he once again set out for the synagogue, somewhat miffed by the fact that this was the first time in all his religious years that he had left home unequipped to face the Succos prayers. The entire delay had cost him some twenty minutes and he wondered what he had done to deserve such a nuisance.

Continuing along his traditional route toward the shul, he noticed ahead of him a non-Jewish woman standing at the side of the road. In the gutter alongside her lay a fist-sized object wrapped in something pink, which she was carefully examining with the toe of her shoe. After concluding that the object had little nutritional or pecuniary value to her, she shrugged her shoulder and continued on her way. Struck by that natural instinct which, according to the adage, tends to get cats into more trouble than they care for, Harold once again altered his course and headed across the street to have his curiosity satiated. Much to his surprise, there in the gutter lay a healthy yellow *esrog*, complete with protective cover and all the other vital appendages. Assuming that the *esrog's* owner was a member of his own congregation, he picked it up and resolved in his mind to have an announcement made in the shul in an attempt to reunite the mislaid citron with its no-doubt grieving owner.

As he approached the synagogue building, Harold noticed a figure exiting the shul premises appearing distinctly shaken. The look of angst on the man's face changed rapidly to one of glee as the figure noticed the pink shape in Harold's hand. Suddenly, Harold felt his load being lifted off his shoulders as he stepped confidently forward and presented the *esrog* to its rightful owner, the very same man who had placed the vital order which had helped put Harold's business on its feet. A debt of gratitude had been repaid in a most unexpected way.

Harold had "toiled," and in the end he "found."

▪ Shabbos Arrangements

There is an age-old tradition to eat fish on Shabbos. One of the reasons given is that, as is well known, several species of fish sustain themselves by consuming other fish, often by chasing after them and swallowing them whole. Considering this state of affairs, it would seem that the prey of carnivorous fish would be lying inside the stomach with its tail at the back and its head facing forward, in the position it had been in when it was swallowed. In reality, however, evidence indicates otherwise. Upon opening any carnivorous fish, one finds its prey lying head to tail, as if it were swallowed head first! This would indicate that the smaller fish had been traveling toward the larger one when it was consumed.

What this fact represents is that although the larger fish expends effort in chasing after smaller fish, in the end the prey that it succeeds in catching is that fish that "just happened" to be coming toward it.

This parable perfectly sums up the endeavors of a human being, for although he expends a large amount of effort "chasing" after his livelihood, what he brings home at the end of the month is only what Hashem sends his way (Apiryon, as quoted by Lekach Tov).

This perspective is a critical one if one wishes to observe Shabbos properly, for if one understands it, it will be far easier to close the doors of one's business each Friday afternoon. The following story was told to me by Rabbi Menachem Raff.

It was a classic tale of reversed fortunes. Issie Glassman spent the early part of the 20th century making vast amounts of money. He mixed in high society, and his wholesale business was renowned as one of the most prestigious in Johannesburg. On the opposite extreme, his friend Louis Raff was barely eking out a living. The small gas station that he had set up not far from Issie's emporium barely supported his family, and every tank of fuel that was sold was cause for a small celebration among Louis's four sons. The men's friendship was one founded on the solid traditions of the *"heim"* (Eastern European homeland), and Issie used every opportunity to try and help out his friend Louis. He lent him money, entered into partnerships with him, and patronized the fledgling filling station.

As the gas station began to succeed and turn a profit, the friendship between the two faded, and by the time Issie passed away, the two had all but lost contact. In the ensuing years, Louis Raff slowly developed his filling station into a thriving concern, while Issie's store was slowly run into the ground as his son Steven tried valiantly to fend off opportunistic and thieving clients. Within a few short years, Steven was earning a meager salary selling secondhand cars for someone. One family had climbed the ladder of good fortune, while the second had come tumbling down.

Not long after the demise of the Glassman business, a wealthy businessman rented a piece of Louis Raff's filling station and set up a secondhand-car showroom. Knowing that his old friend's son was in need of a better job, Louis arranged that Steven Glassman would work at the showroom, at a vastly better salary than he was earning before. It was a tiny repayment for all that Steven's father had done for Louis in his time of need.

Within a short time, Steven had turned the used-car showroom into a thriving concern, and he was slowly given more and more control over the business. Unfortunately, the wealthy businessman who owned it became greedy, and began drawing large amounts of funds out of the business. It was not long before he had milked the business dry, and the still profitable concern had accrued a massive debt. The businessman eventually agreed to take some of his debts and move on, leaving Steven the option of picking up the remainder of the debts and taking over the business.

The knock at the Raffs' door was not unexpected, for they knew that Steven did not have sufficient funds to restart the business.

After some intense negotiation, Louis Raff agreed to take over the business and its debts, with Steven Glassman at the helm. It was Steven's lucky break, and he was anxious to prove himself. There was, however, one condition Louis made with the young Glassman. Although Steven was not an observant Jew at the time, the Raffs were, and at their insistence he committed himself to not trading or doing any business on Shabbos or *Yom Tov*. The business was to be Sabbath observant, even if its director was not. The deal was struck on *erev* Rosh Hashanah, and they called the showroom "Rosh Hashanah Motors."

Steven was very eager to prove his worth to his newfound benefactors, and his eagerness paid off. Within a short time, the business was once again showing a small profit. Steven set himself sales goals, and consistently met them at every month's end.

Until February. Then came the lean month when nothing seemed to move. He tried every trick in the book but was consistently disappointed. The end of the month neared, but his sales goals seemed miles away.

It was a Friday morning close to the end of the month when a man strode into the showroom. By then Steven was an expert at judging his customers, and knew exactly where to direct the well-dressed, confident-looking executive. Although Rosh Hashanah Motors did not regularly stock top-of-the-line vehicles, Steven happened to have a low-mileage Lexus in excellent condition on the floor at the time, and it was to that corner that he directed his flamboyant customer. Long before a customer even opens his mouth a good salesman can judge whether a sale will be made or not, and Steven was smiling inwardly, because suddenly it looked like he might just meet the month's sales goal after all.

His pitch was well directed and it focused on the man's need for the exceptional comfort that the vehicle could offer. The only snag was when the man inquired about what sum he could get for trading in his present vehicle. Steven regretted having to take the trade-in, but agreed anyway without flinching. He knew that even if he lost some money on the trade-in, his profit would still be sufficient to just meet his month-end sales target.

Steven was certain that the deal was all tied up, until the man informed him that he would be returning the following day to pick up the car. Steven's heart sank. He hesitated for a moment and then, with superhuman self-control, informed the man that he was not open on Saturdays but that he would be available first thing Sunday morning. The man seemed slightly dubious, and halfheartedly agreed to come back only on Monday, as he would be unavailable on Sunday.

The weekend passed agonizingly slowly for Steven, and when the phone call finally came in on Monday morning, his worst fears were confirmed. The man had found a similar car on Saturday, and the deal was off.

Steven was shattered by the news. It was clear to him that it was only because he had observed the Shabbos in the face of great odds that he had lost the deal. With a heavy heart he went to tell Louis what had happened.

The response of the Raffs was an eye-opener for him, for it seemed obvious to his religious friends that the entire episode was simply a test of Steven's steadfastness to his commitment. Nevertheless, this attitude did little to console Steven over the lost sale and the missed sales goal.

Two days later, a customer walked into the showroom, and with hardly any fuss, bought the Lexus: A clean sale. Without a trade-in. And making the month.

▪ Cased

One of the most well-known and well-used philosophical dilemmas is often couched in the almost rhetorical question, "Why do bad things happen to good people?" It is amusing to note that the question is seldom posed in the converse form, for few people are troubled by the inevitably decadent and immoral billionaire uncle. What troubles people more is why they must go through hard times, and also why their apparently decent friends and relatives suffer.

One answer to this question lies in the definitions of the terms "good people" and "bad things." In all cases pertaining to other people, we are almost never in a position to judge these two factors, for only G-d sees whether a person is good or bad. Furthermore, what is often perceived as a "bad thing" will turn out in the most positive way imaginable. The following story is a more obvious example of this idea, and was told to me not long ago by the person involved.

Moty Kotzen's business has owed its existence to a series of miracles which have occurred from the moment of his taking the helm. When the middle-aged father of four inherited the shell of a company, he was completely oblivious to the fact that a certain financier in Johannesburg had a twenty-year-old contract with the company. This contract entitled the financier to confiscate any of the company's assets in the event that the company owed him money. A few months into his first year of business, Moty unwittingly borrowed a sum from the financier, and when the time came to repay the loan, Moty did not have the funds available. The man produced the aging contract and set into motion the legal proceedings to commandeer Moty's newly acquired company. By some incredible twist of fate, coupled with some hard work on the part of a dedicated lawyer friend, Moty succeeded in warding off the takeover bid and in the process managed to win a large sum in damages. That was how things began for him, and it was a portent of the way the company would survive for many years to come.

Moty describes how, over the years, the ideas which to him seemed to be market bestsellers inevitably flopped dismally, and just when things seemed on the verge of collapse, a product would surface from the most improbable source and tide the company over for another few months. The following incident is just one remarkable example of the open Divine intervention Moty has seen over the years.

Moty's company manufactures suitcases and tote bags. As with many other similar products, there are periods during the year which are slower than others, and it was during one of these lean phases that Moty was approached by a representative of one of the large manufacturing operations in South Africa. The company specializes in hi-tech equipment, and was launching a new line of portable printers onto the international market. The promotion had a tight deadline, and they urgently needed a custom-made tote bag for the product, hence the call. Moty could barely conceal his glee, because almost predictably, the order of thirty thousand bags had arrived just in time to help him cover a large debt he owed to an overseas supplier. He readily accepted the contract and set about designing the bag to fit the sample printer provided by the manufacturer.

Within a few short weeks, thirty thousand bags were ready and were delivered to the manufacturer's forwarding office to be sent to America in time for the promotion. Payment for the bags was due to Moty on the 15th day of the month of delivery.

The day of the 15th dawned long after Moty arrived at the factory, for he was accustomed at the time to rise extremely early to unlock the doors for the first shift. Having settled a few pressing matters, Moty went to *daven Shacharis* after leaving explicit instructions with his secretary that he not be disturbed. While Moty was *davening*, a man appeared in the reception area asking to see him. The secretaries were by then very familiar with their boss's prayer habits, and informed the man that he would be available in about half an hour. The man explained that his visit concerned an extremely urgent matter, and he attempted to coerce the secretaries into reaching Moty, but to no avail. He paced the waiting room agitatedly as he waited.

Half an hour later, Moty entered the reception area of his office to find a distraught and pale-looking gentleman in the waiting room. He recognized him instantly as the man who had placed the massive bag order, the man who was supposed to bring him a large sum of money which was to keep his company treading water for another few months. Moty's heart skipped a beat. *What could possibly be the matter?* he wondered to himself. The representative did not leave him in suspense for long. "The bags are all wrong!" he blurted.

As the words left the man's mouth, Moty felt his heart tumbling through his very being. His mind raced out of control, calculating how he was going to break the catastrophic news to his wife and employees. His company could not survive this blow. In his mind, he was already running through the liquidation procedures, wondering how long the whole process would take and how much he could rescue for himself. A second later he snapped out of his shocked reverie. "What exactly is the matter with them?" he asked shakily.

"I'm not quite sure how this happened," the man explained, "but our product does not seem to fit in your bag. Our American representative sent the whole lot back." Moty reeled and invited the man into his office. The two entered the room determined to work out what had gone wrong. Inwardly, Moty knew that he had designed the bag to fit the sample, and that his design procedure was nearly flawless. With rising hopes, he showed the man the sample printer that he had been given to work from and demonstrated how it fit into the bag perfectly. Suddenly, the man slapped his head in frustration. "I've got it!" he exclaimed angrily. "The fools who sent you the sample left out the lid!"

That day, Moty received payment for the thirty thousand bags, all of which were scrapped by the client. Later, he entered into a second agreement with him to remake the entire order, only this time at a 50-percent premium due to the urgency of the contract.

Moty paid his debts and the business survived, and continues to do so until today. But like all other businesses, it is really only "by the grace of G-d."

fter contravening the instruction of Hashem and consuming the fruit of the Tree of Knowledge, the Torah tells us that Adam and his wife Chavah heard the voice of Hashem moving through the garden, and they hid from Him among the trees. The verse then tells us:

"And Hashem Elokim called out to the man and said to him, 'Ayekah — Where are you?'"

Throughout the ages, people have experienced hardships in their lives, and tragically their response has often been to question, "Where is G-d at this time of difficulty?" It has been the cry of the faithless for generations. Ironically, this call has been preempted for centuries and millennia by the call of the Creator who wants to know "Ayekah? — Where are you?"

The midrash poignantly sums up this concept with the following parable: A father and son once set out on a journey. The father hoisted his son onto his shoulders and they were on their way. A few miles on, the son noticed from his high vantage point an item lying on the ground and he said, "Father, pick it up and give it to me." The father complied with the request and handed the item up to his son, and they continued on their way. Presently, the son noticed yet another object which aroused his youthful curiosity and once again the father passed the item up to the little boy at his request. This pattern continued throughout the journey. Some time later, they passed a wayfarer on the road. As the man approached, the little boy called out to the man, "Excuse me, sir." The man stopped. "Have you seen my father?" the boy inquired. When the father heard his son's question, he shouted to the boy, "Do you not know where I am?" Without any further ado, the father hoisted the child off his shoulders and placed him on the ground. Moments later a dog came and bit the child (*Shemos Rabbah* 36:2).

We have to perpetually remind ourselves that as we push our way through the journey of life, we are being guided and looked after. We must guard ourselves from forgetting that we too are riding on our Father's shoulders.

The stories which follow are of people who made epic journeys, people who realized that they were riding on their Father's shoulders.

▪ By Accident

The Jewish nation finally stood before Sinai, ready to receive the Torah. It was an earth-shattering moment, when a once-downtrodden nation was launched through the final stage of their redemption and was formed into a chosen people, to be the bearers of the infinite Torah with its sweeping universal implications. It was perhaps the defining moment, the climax of the formation of our illustrious nation, and an event which redefined the nature and function of the entire world.

Considering the significance of the event, one would have expected the portion in which it is found in the Torah to bear an equally grand title. Perhaps simply "Torah" or "Sinai" would have been appropriate, or maybe even "Moshe," after our heroic leader and conveyor of the treasured Torah. Why, then, is the parashah *describing the giving of the Torah named after Yisro — the Midyanite priest of idol worship and one-time adviser to the hated Pharaoh? What did he do to merit such an honor, that this most cherished* parashah *is named after him?*

Rashi *tells us that it was the reports about the splitting of the Sea of Reeds and the subsequent battle the Israelites fought with the Amalekites that inspired Yisro to track down his son-in-law in the desert. The commentators observe that what made Yisro unique was not that he heard about these miraculous events, for they were common knowledge. Yisro's greatness was attributed to the way he responded to the news, that he chose to come and join the Jewish nation.*

Although the Jewish nation may appear to be elitist and xenophobic, the exact opposite is true. Any non-Jewish person who sincerely desires to accept the responsibilities and obligations which bind a practicing Jew is welcomed into the fold with open arms. It is only to discourage those gentiles who are not sincere that we shun converts when they first approach us. The ultimate example of this was Yisro, who demonstrated his commitment to Hashem, and was prepared to drop everything in order to respond to his calling. This is perhaps one of the reasons this parashah *is called "Yisro," for he symbolizes the universal accessibility of the Torah to anyone who sincerely desires it.*

Every ordinary person at some stage in his or her life experiences moments of inspiration. Great people act on those moments. Yisro heard, he came, and he converted. The following story tells us of someone who heard his calling, responded to it, and was welcomed into the fold.

"One who comes upon a place where he experienced a miracle should say, 'Blessed are You, Hashem, Who made a miracle for me in this place'" (Berachos 9).

While teaching this idea from the Talmud, Rabbi Moshe Berman, a well-known Johannesburg rabbi and teacher, related the following incident which involved himself and his family. What is remarkable about this story is that for the Berman family, what occurred was a true miracle, yet for the other young man involved, it proved to be the major turning point in his life.

Traditionally, the three-week period between the 17th of Tammuz and the 9th of Av is a time of misfortune for the Jewish people. Many tragic chapters of our history began during this period, including the destruction of both our Temples, the Spanish Inquisition, and numerous other troubles. It is for this reason that many have a custom not to travel during what has become known as "The Three Weeks," while the national *mazal* is at its lowest.

Rabbi Berman was maintaining a hectic teaching schedule, and he realized that whenever he would take his family on vacation, it would impact on his students' Torah study. The only time he could take off without affecting his teaching too much was during "The Three Weeks." The family desperately needed to get away together, and considering that it was for the sake of his students' Torah studies, the Rabbi eventually decided that they should go, despite the time of year.

A few days prior to their departure, a colleague told Rabbi Berman about a small private game reserve in the Eastern Transvaal province. This reserve was, according to the colleague, one of the few places in the world where one could stand the chance of spotting a white lion, a very rare and beautiful creature seldom seen in the wild. On this advice, the Bermans booked a stay at iNgwalala.

On Sunday morning, 18 Tammuz, they left Johannesburg, stopping to spend the night on a small farm along the way. The next morning, Monday, they set out early to complete the final leg of their journey into the heart of the African bush. After a short while, the route took them off the main road and onto what appeared to be an ordinary gravel road. They drove for what seemed like an eternity, until they felt as if they had traversed half the country on this meandering track which could scarcely be called a road.

Eventually, a farmer flagged them down and asked them where they were heading. On hearing that they were heading for iNgwalala, the farmer let out a low whistle and peered at the horizon, as if to say they were searching on the wrong continent. He then rattled off a complex set of directions, recommending that they not go back the way they had come; rather, since they were already so far off course, they should head off in an entirely new direction which would hopefully bring them safely at iNgwalala's front gate. Once again the Bermans rattled and bumped their way along another dirt road, trailing a large cloud of dust behind them.

For twenty minutes they drove along this road without seeing a single sign of human civilization, as if they had not only traveled into the countryside, but had also traveled back two hundred years in time. Baboons frolicked on the side of the road, and other wild animals skittered into the bush as the car rattled past. They noticed that the road they were traveling on had actually once been tarred, and had become completely covered with loose sand from disuse. A vague feeling of loneliness crept over the family.

A bend suddenly loomed in front of them. The car tried valiantly to follow the curve of the road. The tires scrabbled for grip. The car careened violently off course, skidded off the edge of the road, and came to rest upside down in a shallow ditch.

The dust settled, and for a few seconds silence reigned. Then the children began screaming.

Rabbi Berman heard the sound of his wife's voice, calling from the seat next to him. Behind him, the children were crying hysterically. Miraculously, neither his wife nor any of the children were hurt. They all pulled themselves free of the car. Rabbi Berman, however, was in tremendous pain from a wound to his head, from which he was losing copious amounts of blood. Once out of the car, he wrapped his head with a piece of clothing and took stock of the situation, which appeared hopeless.

Miraculously, he was the only one hurt. However, the car was damaged beyond repair, and they had no means of communicating their plight to the outside world. Walking was out of the question — his head wound made sure of that — and besides, they didn't have a clue how far it would be to the next human habitation. With no other option, they huddled together on the side of the road beside the upturned car and began to recite *Tehillim*. Silently, Rabbi Berman mouthed *Viduy*, the confession a person says just prior to death.

Four minutes later, a cloud of dust indicated the approach of a car and the answer to their prayers. They watched the car's progress eagerly, and a few moments later the young driver skidded his Jeep to a halt and jumped out to see what had happened. He took one look at the Rabbi's wound, and then went into action. He lifted Rabbi Berman carefully and laid him down on the front seat of the Jeep. Then, he helped the rest of the family into the back. Once everyone was in, he hopped into the driver's seat and floored the gas. He instructed Rabbi Berman to keep talking to him so as not to lose consciousness, while he tried to find his way to the Hoedspruit military hospital. From his tone of voice, Rabbi Berman understood that this, too, would require a small miracle.

At the hospital, a still-conscious Rabbi Berman was rushed into the operating room. There his condition was stabilized by the attending doctors who then placed him in an ambulance and dispatched him to Johannesburg for urgent attention. The ambulance attendants were instructed to monitor the Rabbi's state of consciousness closely, and were told by the doctors that should they notice any signs of deterioration, they should stop immediately at the nearest hospital for treatment. Rabbi Berman described afterwards how he painfully wrote his will on the back of an x-ray envelope as they rushed toward Johannesburg. He also described how, as they drove, he reviewed in his mind the book of *Shir HaShirim*, the poignantly beautiful song describing the affection and love between Hashem and the Jewish nation, and how after that experience he would never forget the song for the rest of his life.

At one point along the way, the ambulance personnel thought Rabbi Berman was losing consciousness. They stopped at the nearest town, where they found the local hospital filled to capacity as a result of a major bus accident which had occurred in the area. They continued towards Johannesburg. Once there, the

Rabbi was admitted to one of the local private clinics where, with the help of some expert doctors, he staged a miraculous recovery. It was not long before he was discharged from the hospital, safely on the road to recovery.

A week later the Bermans' phone rang in Johannesburg. The young man on the line had a vaguely familiar voice, albeit tainted by a heavy Afrikaans accent. He wanted urgently to speak with Rabbi Berman. When Rabbi Berman came to the phone the young man introduced himself as Anton Wessels, the man with the Jeep who had helped them at the accident site, and who had contributed to saving Rabbi Berman's life. "I've come up to Johannesburg," said the man, "because I need to see you urgently." Rabbi Berman was taken aback. The journey from the Eastern Transvaal takes between five and six hours; it was obvious that this man had something important on his mind. They arranged a time to meet.

When the man arrived at the Rabbi's house, he was welcomed and led to the Rabbi's study. This is the story he told:

"I grew up on a farm together with my family, who are Afrikaans-speaking and devout Christians. In my youth, the road on which you had your accident was the main road through the district. We used to travel that road often. As I grew up, the road was bypassed by other newer ones and we slowly stopped using that road, as did most of the farmers in the area.

"I am now 20 years old, and three weeks ago I completed my national service with the South African Defense Force. While in the army, I had a chance to look back on my life, and to remember the good times of my youth. Somewhere along the line I remembered the road you were traveling on, and I made a decision to go and revisit the road of my childhood, to relive all the memories. Something of a pilgrimage, if you know what I mean.

"For two weeks I procrastinated, each day another distraction keeping me from my mission. Last Monday I finally got around to making the trip. That is how I came to find you."

He paused for a moment to let his words sink in, and then continued:

"You should also be aware that not long ago there was another accident along that stretch of road. It wasn't until two weeks later that the battered car was found. Its occupants weren't as lucky as you. They waited for help which never arrived. You must realize that if I had decided to set out on my trip of nostalgia even a half-hour earlier, you could still be waiting there now. If I would have set out a half-hour later, you probably would not have survived your wounds."

The man studied the Rabbi carefully as he continued talking.

"I have never been a very religious man. I've never given much thought to the events that occur in the world. After this whole business, however, I have seen that someone was looking after you, and I have decided that I would like to know more about the difference between Jews and gentiles. I would like to know what my responsibilities are."

For the next few hours, Rabbi Berman sat with this young man and reviewed with him the history of Christianity and Judaism. He then went on to explain to him what his obligations and responsibilities were as a non-Jew. Despite Rabbi Berman's attempts at dissuading him, within a few weeks Anton Wessels became adamant that he wanted to become a Jew. One time, when Rabbi Berman had business to attend to in Israel, Anton Wessels accompanied him there in order to discover even more about what it means to be a Jew. Once in Israel, Rabbi Berman took the young man to meet some of the Sages and Torah leaders of the generation. Anton was truly captivated by all he discovered. Within three years he converted to Judaism and began attending one of the great yeshivos in Jerusalem, plumbing the depths of the holy Torah.

Rabbi Berman ended off his story by saying that he often had the desire to return to the exact spot on that deserted road so that he could make the blessing, "Who made a miracle for me in this place."

Anton would probably feel the same way.

▪ Pintele Yid, Giant Jew

"...If the purpose of the creation of man was to function in this world, it would not have been necessary to inject into him a neshamah *which is so significant and elevated. And not only is it more elevated than the angels themselves, but it will not find any satisfaction whatsoever from all of the pleasures of this world...*

"To what can this be compared? To a [simple] city dweller who married the daughter of the king. Whatever he would bring her would be meaningless because she is the daughter of the king. Similarly, if you bring the soul all the pleasures of this world, they would be meaningless. Why? Because she is exalted" (Introduction to Mesilas Yesharim*).*

Inside every Jew burns a neshamah *which will never be satisfied if not sustained with the right "food." An unhappy* neshamah *will tug at the person until eventually he takes the necessary steps and treats it to the kind of fare that it desires. What follows is one of the most moving stories I have ever heard, about a most remarkable individual. I tracked him down, and this is the story he told me.*

The Orange Free State forms the core of the South African geographical landscape, a vast and uncluttered region bounded on the east by the towering slopes of the Drakansberg and the mountainous kingdom of Lesotho. It is a province which boasts its own unique beauty, a beauty which arises from its simplicity and absence of pretentiousness, and a region which would seem to have gotten its name from its most significant yet ephemeral landmark, the spectacular and inspiring sunsets over its glowing grasslands. As one crosses from the more cosmopolitan Gauteng province into the Orange Free State, a sign invites one to "Come to the Free State and discover your soul." Some cynics interpret this sign to mean that there is not much else to be discovered there, but in truth it is an achingly beautiful part of the country, where the silence and simplicity can indeed act as a mirror to the soul.

The city of Bloemfontein, judicial capital of the Republic of South Africa, lies in the heart of the Orange Free State, making the city in some ways the center of the Republic. It was in Bloemfontein — or "Bloem" as it is affectionately known by many South Africans — that a young man by the name of Stan Cohen was born and raised, together with his three brothers. Despite his parents' indifference to their Jewish background, Stan and his brothers were sent to *cheder*, which was the prevailing custom at the time. Shul was attended very intermittently, and by the time Stan was in his teens, he had stopped attending synagogue services altogether.

At age 21, Stan met a young woman who agreed to accompany him through life, and on the basis of this arrangement the two were soon happily married. The fact that Marie was not Jewish did not trouble Stan at all, for he had been brought up unaware of the significance of such matters. Shortly after their nuptials, Stan commenced his tertiary education, and within a few years was qualified as a motor mechanic. Time passed and the young couple decided to move out of the big city. When Stan was offered a small-town position as a motor-mechanics lecturer, he hastily grabbed at the opportunity, and the two soon found themselves in the town of Ficksburg, on the border between the Free State and Lesotho. This move turned out to be a temporary one, and before long, they once again relocated.

The town of Jacobsdal can be found only on a detailed map of the Orange Free State, some 150 kilometers west of Bloemfontein, midway between the city of Kimberly and the town of Koffiefontein. It was here that the Cohens finally settled, and where Stan once again found a position lecturing on the workings of the automobile and its repair. It was here too that Stan and Marie brought their two children, a daughter and a son, into the world, and set about raising them as upstanding members of society.

By the time Stan arrived in Jacobsdal, he had spent close to half a lifetime in the Orange Free State, and he admitted to identifying himself far more with the Afrikaans nation than with his Jewish forebears. In fact, Stan perceived himself as an Afrikaaner who just happened to have been born Jewish. In Jacobsdal, Stan made an attempt to assimilate even further from his Jewish roots, although he later conceded that this was to no avail, for he was never entirely accepted by the Afrikaans community.

As time passed and Stan watched his children grow up, something began to burn deep inside the *neshamah* of this middle-aged Jew adrift in the culture and lifestyle of a small Free State town. Gradually he found himself taking interest in people involved in religious pursuits, and he became fascinated by the concept of prayer. He felt that something needed to change in his lifestyle, but he was not sure what it was.

One day, Stan traveled to the nearby city of Kimberly to purchase some supplies not available in Jacobsdal. There, he headed directly to Klein's general store, a bustling concern owned and run by the Klein brothers. Having completed his purchases, Stan was about to exit the shop when Philip Klein, the manager, called him back. "Cohen, did you say?" he inquired of his somewhat bewildered client. "Are you by any chance Jewish?" It was a question which Stan had avoided for many years, but one which he suddenly felt happy to answer. "Indeed I am, Mr. Klein, but why do you ask?"

Replied the shopkeeper: "Well, Mr. Cohen, I wanted to invite you to try out our shul. We run regular services there and are always on the lookout for new members."

It was an offer which Stan would have laughed at a few years previously, yet the next Saturday, Stan found himself standing outside the Kimberly shul. He paced the sidewalk outside the shul for a few minutes, too intimidated to go in. It was only when he spied his newfound friend Philip Klein walking in that he mustered up the courage to enter. After nearly thirty years, Stan had finally returned. It was a strange experience for the middle-aged man, and although he knew that he was doing the right thing, it also felt tremendously foreign.

That Saturday was the beginning of a gradual but steady renaissance in Stan's life, a period of years during which he slowly rediscovered his roots and set about the long and difficult process of awakening the slumbering Jew which had lain dormant inside of him for many years. It was an arduous task, but one which was exciting and liberating for the man who had for so long languished in the small town of Jacobsdal in the Orange Free State. He attended the synagogue services in Kimberly regularly, and developed a close friendship with the local rabbi, who he enlisted to teach him the rudiments of Jewish law and lifestyle.

As Stan slowly blossomed and changed, he often wondered what his rediscovered Jewishness meant to his marriage, considering that his wife was not Jewish and, consequently, neither were his children. It was a question which always left him faintly uneasy but one which he was never confident enough or motivated enough to confront. After a while, Stan had grown as much as was possible in the little town, and as so often happens, he settled into the rut of routine and complacency.

When telling his story, Stan related an incident which occurred to him during this period, as he was walking out of shul one Saturday. It is a bizarre incident, and hence I will recount it in his own words for the sake of the reader's own judgment:

"I had stayed on after the Saturday morning service to listen to a *shiur* on the weekly *parashah*. As I stepped out of the shul into the bright sunlight, I sensed a strange feeling come over me, and suddenly I perceived an unusual apparition, an image which I saw not with my eyes but one which I felt with my senses. In this image I saw darkness opening up in front of me, and in the darkness I perceived what appeared to be a flat gold table. The table was bare; it had nothing on its surface. Then, as suddenly as the image appeared, it was gone. At the time I had no idea what this image could have meant. When I asked the local rabbi, he appeared shocked and told me to leave the entire incident alone. Only later did I learn that a gold table is a common Jewish metaphor for one's share in the Next World. Mine had been bare."

As life chugged along in the little town, Stan's progress stagnated. Then one day, Stan happened upon a book, a book which was to change his life. The book, entitled *A Tzaddik in Our Times*, details the inspiring life and times of one of the previous generation's great Sages and leaders, Rabbi Aryeh Levin. After reading the book, Stan felt something welling up inside of him, a need to raise himself even higher, to learn and to grow and to meet new challenges.

Shortly afterwards, Stan informed his wife that he was going on a trip to Israel. He felt that such a journey would jumpstart his growth process once again, and allow him to capitalize on his newfound inspiration. He managed to secure a place on a pilot tour to the Holy Land, and in December 1994, he drove to Johannesburg and caught his flight. It was a short visit to Israel, but one which made a huge impact on him. From the very moment that he landed there, he felt as if a great hollowness inside of him had been filled, and when he stood in front of the ancient golden stones of the Western Wall, he felt as if he would burst with joy and fulfillment. While in the Holy Land, Stan took advantage of the opportunity to consult with some of the great Sages residing there, asking many of them for advice regarding his situation back at home in Jacobsdal.

At some point during the tour, one of Stan's co-travelers made an unusual suggestion: "Who wants to meet a *tzaddik*?" It was the type of invitation that Stan could not resist and he jumped at the opportunity. The next day found him seated in front of Rabbi Chaim Kanievsky, one of the Torah giants of our generation and son of the late Rabbi Yaakov Yisrael Kanievsky, more commonly known as "the Steipler." With the help of a translator, Stan described his background and the predicament he found himself in back home. Then, he mustered up his courage and told Rabbi Kanievsky of the strange apparition he had perceived while coming out of shul that Saturday morning.

When he had finished, the venerable Rabbi smiled knowingly and told Stan, "Hashem has several rewards for you."

A few days later, Stan boarded the plane back to South Africa with many thoughts and feelings churning inside him. On the one hand, he was excited by his experiences in the Holy Land and the amazing feeling of fulfillment which had come over him while he was there. On the other hand, a heavy feeling of foreboding pervaded him as he considered the frightening challenge that lay ahead.

Stan faced one of the most difficult challenges imaginable. Stan is a *Kohen*. The Jewish law is very strict with regard to whom a *Kohen* may or may not marry. According to these laws, if a *Kohen* was living with a non-Jewess under secular law, he may not subsequently marry her under Jewish law, even if she converts to Judaism. Consider now the terrifying dilemma which Stan faced.

Back in Jacobsdal, Stan was a different man. He stopped eating at the college where he was lecturing, preferring to eat at home where he could ensure that the food was all kosher. Although she did not understand what had come over him, Stan's wife was extremely supportive of his newfound habits. He began taking leave from his job on Saturdays and Jewish festivals. Slowly a plan began forming in his head.

Stan met with a lawyer, who assisted him with the transfer of ownership of his house. Next he sold all of his investments and deposited the money into a special bank account. Then, on what was to be his last day in Jacobsdal, he called over his dear wife and children and explained to them what he had been through. He tried to explain to them what a difficult ordeal it had been and how much his heritage meant to him. He wished to live in the Holy Land, he explained, and he hoped that they understood what he was doing. He then handed his wife the title deeds of the house together with the details of the bank accounts, his pension, and the rights to everything that he had ever owned. With a heavy heart but a spring in his step, Stan left Jacobsdal, with almost nothing to his name except the shirt on his back.

Today Stan lives in Jerusalem. He prays three times a day with a *minyan*, wears *tzitzis* and *tefillin*, and studies Torah regularly. In the beginning he struggled to earn a living, until eventually he found a job selling ice cream in a small store. When the loneliness began to become overwhelming, Hashem sent him his *bashert*, a warm and loving woman who understands what Stan (who now calls himself Tzvi) has been through and who is committed to the growth and Torah goals for which Stan sacrificed so much. Stan states openly that he is certain that she is one of those rewards that Rabbi Kanievsky assured him lay waiting for him.

As I finished listening to Stan's heartbreaking yet inspiring story, I asked him if there were any special requests as to how it should be written.

"Just make sure you put Hashem in there somewhere," he insisted. "He made this all happen, and without Him I wouldn't be here today," he said as he smiled warmly across the small Jerusalem flat at his wife.

▪ A Spark Among the Ashes

Our Sages tell us that Adam HaRishon *had a composite* neshamah *(soul), made up of all the souls that will ever come down to the world. After he sinned by eating from the Tree of Knowledge, much of this* neshamah *was taken from him and was injected over two thousand years later into the Jewish people standing at Mount Sinai. Some remnants of holiness were left over, however, and were scattered among the nations of the world, small glowing sparks among the ashes. Occasionally, one of these sparks which is residing in a gentile body begins to rouse itself, yearning for some holiness. This tug is at times sufficient to pull the gentile toward observing the Torah and* mitzvos, *and the gentile will convert. This is an explanation for the phenomenon of* geirus *(conversion), and illuminates the life stories of numerous people who have made this spiritual journey, including such famous converts as Ruth the Moabite, the famous Sages Shma'ayah and Avtalyon, and Onkelos.*

The following fascinating story offers a slightly different perspective on the above idea. I have written it almost exactly as I heard it from the person concerned, to allow the reader to truly appreciate its implications.

Hannes Petrus was born into the Le Roux family of Johannesburg in the early 1940's. The second of three children, Hannes spent the first few years of his life together with his nonreligious Christian family in the new suburb of Hillbrow, a neighborhood which today has become one of the most highly populated inner-city districts in Africa. Things were different then, however, in the days before the high-rise office buildings of the city center began to clutter the Johannesburg horizon. Hannes has an unusually vivid memory of his early years in the rural neighborhood, of playing in the large heaps of building sand lying alongside the dusty roads, of his friendly neighbors, and of the happy times spent in the company of his older brother and younger sister exploring the surrounding fields.

Unfortunately for Hannes, however, the same extraordinary faculty of recollection ensures that he does not forget a darker part of his otherwise joyous youth, a part which he would have given anything to have had erased and expunged from his psyche. It is an affliction he has had to bear silently for the majority of his life, often unable to talk about it even to his closest friends. For as far back as he can remember, Hannes experienced terrible nightmares. Not the kind of nightmare that you chew over together with your breakfast the morning after, or the kind which you laugh about over dinner with some friends, but rather the type which shakes you dementedly out of your sleep in the darkest part of the night and which leaves you trembling with wide-eyed terror until dawn finally arrives.

Hannes experienced these nightmares almost every night, and although they occasionally varied in content, they nearly always reached the same frightening climax. In almost every dream, Hannes would eventually find himself huddling in a freezing ditch. It would be raining and the night sky would be an inky black color. Hannes was hiding from someone. Inevitably, he would have to leave the ditch, and would find himself lying in a dark, exposed field alongside many similar figures, all of whom appeared dead. Then, a man carrying a rifle would approach the spot where Hannes was lying. In his dream, Hannes would think to himself how all he had to do was feign death. The man will leave you alone, he would say to himself. Then in his dream Hannes would suddenly hear a terrible bang, and he would wake up in terror.

These frightening dreams continued throughout Hannes's childhood and well into his adult life. His older brother Danie shared a room with him for most of their youth, and when Hannes would awaken in the night, Danie knew to place a steady hand on his brother's terrified form. This simple contact was normally enough to calm him.

As time passed and the dreams continued, Hannes stopped talking about them, for he felt that people were becoming skeptical of his stories. He preferred to bear his secret silently, rather than face the ridicule he detected in the hearts of his friends and relatives.

One other experience sticks out in Hannes's mind from his years as a child in Johannesburg. He was playing with his brother in a large heap of sand alongside a dirt road in Hillbrow. Nearby a bus stopped and people began to disembark. Suddenly, Hannes felt a terrible fear grip his throat. A soldier had alighted from the bus and was walking peacefully down the street. Hannes felt himself suffocating with an overwhelming feeling of horror. It was only when the man disappeared over the horizon that Hannes began to calm down. He could never understand or explain his unusual reaction.

When Hannes was 4 years old, his father, who worked as a male nurse in Johannesburg, was offered a position as a first aid officer in a mine in what was then Northern Rhodesia. After some deliberation, his father decided to take the post, and in 1946 the Le Roux family left Johannesburg and settled in the mining town of Kitwe on the lucrative "copper belt" of what is today Zambia. The family adjusted quickly and were soon living comfortably, for the miners and associated professionals living on the copper belt led affluent and cosmopolitan lives. Although the Le Roux family spoke their native Afrikaans at home and in church, the language of choice in all other situations was a high-class English, primarily because teachers were brought from England to teach in the mining schools, and as a result, the children of Kitwe were fully conversant in the language. Hannes spent the majority of his school years in the Kitwe education system. It was only for the last two years of his schooling that his parents decided to send him back to South Africa, and he spent them in a school in the town of Ceres in the Southern Cape. After completing his schooling there, Hannes returned to his family in Kitwe.

Back in Kitwe, Hannes did not take long to decide on a career path. Although he would have enjoyed furthering his education, Hannes could not bring himself to squander his youth in a university, especially considering that there were lucrative jobs available in Kitwe in the mining industry, jobs for which one did not need qualifications. Furthermore, Hannes was keenly aware of the fancy new cars which his friends were driving, and was all too eager to have one himself. Thus, at the age of 19, Hannes took a job in one of the mines near Kitwe, a line of work which he was to stay with for nearly forty years.

Shortly after he began working, Hannes's father bought him his first car, a secondhand Humber Hawkshill. It was Hannes's pride and joy, and it boosted his confidence tremendously. With some cash in his pocket and a smart set of wheels, it was not long before the young man began to contemplate his matrimonial prospects.

During his early years in the Kitwe primary school, Hannes had once noticed a girl chasing another girl and hitting her playfully on the head with a hat. It was a fairly mundane scene yet it was one which had stuck in Hannes's head, and over the years, whenever Hannes had wondered who he was going to marry, the strange image of the girl with the hat popped up from somewhere deep in his subconscious.

In 1962, Hannes mustered up the courage to ask the girl — now a young woman — whose name was Rena Venter, out on a date. Within a short while the two were engaged to be married, and not long after that they tied the knot in a church in Kitwe. The young couple remained in Kitwe for a few years, where there first daughter was born. They named the child Shani, a choice which was to be a source of much amazement in later years.

Not long after their first daughter's arrival, Hannes and Rena caught wanderlust, and moved for a short time to a small town in what is today Namibia, where Hannes found work in a copper mine. It was there that their second daughter, whom they named Tanya, was born. Their stay at the copper mine did not last long, and a short while after Tanya's birth they once again moved, this time to the small town of Kuruman in the South African Cape Province, where Hannes found a job in an asbestos mine. This third move saw the arrival of their third daughter, named Eden by her wandering parents.

It was in Kuruman that Hannes's terrible nightmares began to subside. Although he was still not geographically settled, he felt a degree of emotional peace come over him in the little Northern Cape village. Perhaps it had to do with his growing family, and the stability which came with it. Ironically, however, the disappearance of his nightmares did not allow him to reclaim his sleepless nights. In place of the terror came a new feeling, a sensation which began to once again rob him of slumber. What he began to feel was an intense religious awakening, an unusually powerful drive to get to know more about G-d, to better understand the meaning of life. Many nights he lay awake, disturbed by these sentiments, yet unsure of how to respond to them.

Once again the young Le Roux family did not settle for long. After a short few years in Kuruman in South Africa, Hannes was offered a position in a new field altogether, one which would utilize much of his expertise and experience from his mining years. Thus the family of five moved to western Mozambique where a huge hydroelectric dam was being built. Hannes assisted in the construction of the massive underground tunnels used there to transport the water. When his involvement in that project was over, Hannes once again picked up his family and moved with them back to South Africa, this time to another tunneling project, not far from the Southern Cape town of Franschoek. It was there that Hannes was appointed tunnel foreman, a significant advancement from his previous job, and a position of great responsibility on the 32-km-long tunnel. This time the Le Rouxs settled for longer.

It was while working on the tunnels near Franschoek that Hannes finally decided to act on his religious feelings. He found a small chapel in the town, and together with his wife began to attend regular services.

In 1981, an unusual guest speaker visited the chapel. Hannes had always been fascinated by the State of Israel, and had read prolifically on the subject from the time that he was very young. The guest was a representative of a group called "Christian Action for Israel," a group which supported the Jewish State and lobbied for its continued survival. Hannes listened with growing fascination to the man's description of the tiny country and the troubles it was facing. The man concluded his speech with an invitation to all the congregants to join his organization on a tour of the Holy Land. Hannes needed little convincing, and signed up on the spot.

Thus in the middle of 1981, Hannes bade his family farewell and traveled to Israel with the tour. It was a whirlwind trip which was to leave him a changed man. Three incidents on the trip, however, stood out above the rest.

After a memorable night flight, the Israeli national carrier, El Al, landed at Ben Gurion International Airport. As Hannes threaded his way down the aisle of the aircraft toward the exit, he felt an unusual sensation rising up inside of him. It was only when his feet touched the ground and the feeling washed over him completely, that he was able to place the strange feeling of déjà vu. It was an ancient feeling, one which he had to dig very far back into his past to recollect. It was a feeling which he had experienced years before, during his two years of high school which he had spent away from his parents in the boarding school in Ceres in South Africa.

Due to the great distance between Kitwe, where his family was, and the school in Ceres, Hannes was only able to travel home twice a year, and although he had enjoyed his time in the school, the ache of homesickness never left him for the duration of the two years. Those two visits home each year were all that kept him sane during that time period. The train journey from Ceres to Kitwe took three full days, days filled with excitement on the homeward leg, and ones that seemed to drag on forever. When the train finally approached the station, an overwhelming warmness would begin to spread through him, and when he finally glimpsed his family waiting patiently on the platform, Hannes would feel as if he was going to burst with excitement and sheer happiness.

It was this identical emotion which he experienced as his feet touched the soil of Eretz Yisrael.

That was the first incident. For the entire next week, Hannes and his fellow tourists visited various outlying parts of the country including the Golan and the Negev. It was not until a week later that they set out aboard their tour bus for the capital, the ancient city of Jerusalem.

As the bus threaded its way through the rocky deserts east of Jerusalem, Hannes was relaxing in his seat with his back pressed against the window beside it. Suddenly, someone exclaimed: "Jerusalem!" Hannes digested for a moment what the man had said and then slowly turned his face to the window behind him. As his eyes discerned the golden stones of the legendary city, he felt a lump forming in his throat. Moments later, he felt a tear running down his face, followed by a second and a third, and he pressed his nose against the glass so that none of his fellow passengers would see his unexpected reaction. After a few moments he managed to bring his emotions under control, and was relieved to see that none of the other tourists seemed to have noticed. That was the second incident.

The following Sunday morning was when matters reached their climax. The tour group was staying in a hotel in central Jerusalem, and the day began with a trip to the famous, or perhaps infamous, Yad Vashem Holocaust memorial. Hannes did not get to see much of the museum. Minutes after the tour entered the memorial, Hannes paused in front of one of the pictures, a famous photograph depicting a small boy moments before his execution. As the tour breezed past, Hannes felt himself choking with emotion. He needed air. He rushed from the room into the bright sunlight, unable to contain his overwhelming emotions. He ran away from the building, and only stopped when he found a bench to sit on among some trees. Hannes felt devastated.

It was close to an hour before he was able to rejoin the group, who had by then completed their tour. But something felt different. He studied his companions, and remembered how they had breezed through the memorial, perusing the images as if in the Louvre or some other museum of art, and suddenly he could no longer face his people. It was on that day, the day of the third incident, that Hannes began to question the meaning of his life and, more importantly, he began to question the validity of the faith he had accepted since the day he was born. Hannes would never be the same person again.

On his return to Franschoek, Hannes was reserved and inward, and hesitated to tell his wife about what he had experienced. It was only when she told him of an unusual experience that she had had that he realized that she was meant to know of all that he had been through.

Rena told her husband how, while he was away on the tour, she had attended their chapel services as usual. One day, while sitting in the service, Rena was suddenly overwhelmed with emotion, an unusual occurrence for the normally stoic woman. She could offer no explanation for her feeling, and dismissed it as a freak episode. As Hannes listened to his wife's tale, a chill ran up his spine. He asked her when exactly her incident had happened. His suspicion was correct.

Rena's episode had occurred at the very same moment that Hannes was suffering through his ordeal at the Holocaust memorial, on the other side of the world.

At that moment, the couple realized that whatever was occurring in their lives, they were in it together. Hannes told his wife of all that had happened to him while on his tour, and together they resolved to take the matter further.

Thus in 1981, their search for the truth began. It was not long before they moved once again, this time to a platinum mine alongside the town of Rustenburg, an hour out of Johannesburg. It was here that another remarkable incident occurred, one which was to prove significant in the middle-aged couple's religious renaissance. Hannes had taken an interest in the use of HAM radios, a type of high-powered transmitter and receiver which allows amateur operators to communicate over great distances. The amateur radio community is close knit and friendly, and although the members are scattered throughout various parts of the world, many great friendships have developed among them. One day, as Hannes trawled the airwaves, he came across a man named Shlomo Lansky, who lived in the Orange Free State city of Kimberly. After chatting with the man for a few minutes, Hannes heard to his great surprise that his newfound friend was in fact a rabbi. It was the beginning of a close friendship, one which was of great significance in carrying Hannes and Rena through the difficult years that followed. It is a relationship that Hannes treasures to this very day.

In 1992, Hannes once again traveled to Israel with an organized tour. By this time, however, he was beginning to see the warmth and sincerity of the Jewish way of life, and he did not hesitate to voice his opinions on the subject to anyone on the tour who was prepared to listen. This did not gain him favor in the eyes of the predominantly Christian tour organizers, but he soon developed a small following of co-travelers, who clamored to hear what he had to say about the various places and people the tour came across.

On his return to South Africa, Hannes once again made contact with Rabbi Lansky. Hannes had made up his mind and there was not much that was going to stop him. After some intensive discussion, Hannes and Rena set into motion the process of converting to Judaism. The *Beis Din* in Johannesburg agreed to give the couple an extended preparation period of six years, and in 1994 Hannes and Rena began learning about what it means to be Jew.

It was a long and trying process. For the festivals and High Holidays, Hannes took leave from his work on the mine, and the

Le Rouxs traveled down to Kimberly to spend the time with the Lansky family. (It was in Rabbi Lansky's home that Hannes and Rena met a remarkable man by the name of Stan Cohen, who remains a great friend of theirs to this very day. See the story ("*Pintele Yid*").

At first Hannes was fortunate in that he was able to structure his workweek in such a way that from Friday afternoon until Sunday evening he was free from his duties at the mine, and he was thus able to observe Shabbos. After a short while, however, new management took over and began to put pressure on Hannes to work over the weekend as well. When he refused, he was eventually dismissed. During the ensuing legal wrangle, he was able to prove that it was an unfair dismissal, and he was paid a sum of money by the company as compensation. It was more of a moral victory than a financial one, although the lump sum did allow Hannes the luxury of focusing on his studies and the conversion process.

On the seventh of Sivan in the year 5761 (2001), Hannes and Rena were finally accepted by the Johannesburg *Beis Din* into the Jewish nation. It was a moment of triumph and great emotion, the final stage on a long and difficult journey for them. Thereafter, Hannes, who now goes by the name Shimon, applied himself with great fervor to the challenge of mastering the Hebrew language, and three months after his conversion he stood up in the shul and recited the *maftir* and *haftarah*. It was at that moment that he felt that he had truly arrived.

Incidentally, three of the people who traveled to Israel with Shimon on his second tour have also converted. Two live in Cape Town, while the third has now immigrated to Israel. While on that tour, it was those three who were Shimon's finest audience, constantly listening to what he had to say, fascinated by his views on the Jewish people and the Holy Land. Interestingly enough, Shimon's brother has also since converted to Judaism, as has his niece. Shimon and Rena intend to make *aliyah* themselves within the near future.

This could be where Shimon's story ends, a remarkable story of a man and his wife who responded to a powerful calling, and who persevered until the very end, influencing many others along the way. There is, however, a further twist to Shimon's story, one which adds a frightening dimension to what has transpired through this amazing man's life. I present the details as he related them to me, and will leave the interpretation up to the reader.

Although Shimon's terrifying nightmares had stopped entirely after his conversion, he could never come to terms with what they meant and why they had recurred with such unusual frequency. What troubled him also was the fact that it was always the same dream — the ditch, the freezing field with the inert bodies, and the sound of shooting. What did it all mean?

Shortly after their conversion, Shimon and Rena were invited to a Shabbos meal at the home of one of the congregants of their shul. Over lunch, Shimon described to some of the people present the terrible nightmares which he had had in his youth, also mentioning to them how puzzled he was by the experiences. After the meal, a woman who had been at the table approached him. She had listened with fascination to his story, and thought that she could offer an explanation to his unusual experiences. She referred him to a book that she had read, insisting that it would answer some of his questions. Shimon located the book and had it sent to him.

What he read in it changed his life. The book told the true stories of numerous people who had suffered similar torment to what Shimon had experienced. The book proposed a chilling explanation. These people, the author suggested, were possibly the souls of Jews who had died in the Holocaust, who were reincarnated.

After reading the book, Shimon is a changed man. No longer is he disturbed by the dreams that he experienced in his past. He believes that this hypothesis can explain his unusual reaction to the sight of the soldier when he was a little child, and his overwhelming emotions on his visit to Yad Vashem. Shimon has come to terms with who he is, and why he is Jewish today. He feels that the circle has finally closed.

Shimon had been born in 1942, at the height of the Holocaust

▪ The Journey

There is a well-known legend told about a kindhearted man who visited Jerusalem some fifteen hundred years ago. Appalled by the dire living conditions of the Jewish residents of the Holy City, the man undertook to raise funds to ease their burdens. He set out for the wealthy city of Baghdad together with a caravan of travelers in the hope of finding a few philanthropic Jews in the city to contribute toward his cause. Prior to their departure, the man arranged with the caravan leader that the caravan would stop on Shabbos to allow him to observe the day of rest appropriately. However, when Friday afternoon arrived, the caravan leader laughed at the notion and instructed the camel drivers to proceed. Without any hesitation, the G-d-fearing man dismounted from his steed and set about preparing for Shabbos alone in the desert. The story describes how after a short while he sensed that he was not alone, and he looked up to see a large lion padding toward him. After his initial shock, the man sensed that the lion meant him no harm, and he proceeded with his Shabbos activities with the large cat studying him from a distance. That night, the lion slept nearby, and when Shabbos finally drew to a close with the appearance of the stars in the nighttime sky on the next evening, the lion approached the man and crouched beside him. The man climbed onto its back, and the lion raced across the sands until they caught up with the caravan. The man's fellow travelers watched in awe as he walked through the camp with the lion by his side. Thereafter, he was treated with great reverence, and on his arrival in Baghdad he succeeded in raising a large sum of money for the people of Jerusalem. From then on, the man was known as Ariel, or "the lion of G-d."

What follows is an extraordinary story told to me by the person in question, a modern-day story with some remarkable similarities to the tale of the kindhearted traveler simply known as "Ariel."

Mussi Dawa does not know his own age. What he does know, however, is that he was born in the early 70's in the strife-torn regions of Northern Ethiopia, close to where the country now shares a border with Eritrea. Eritrea lies on the Red Sea, and is today an independent country. Back then, however, Eritrea was but a province of Ethiopia, fiercely fighting for its sovereignty. Since 1961 when Eritrea first demanded its independence, the two countries have been locked in a bloody war which has cost thousands of lives and which has prevented the region from seeing any marked economic prosperity.

Not long after the start of the war, Mussi was drafted into the Ethiopian army. He estimates that he was between 12 and 13 years old at the time. The use of children as soldiers has become a trademark of these ugly African wars, and the image of a waif barely old enough to be in elementary school toting a large automatic machine gun has become a poignant symbol of the oppression and misery which inevitably surrounds these conflicts. Mussi relates that there are numerous stories of children who have died in airless refrigerators and cupboards, where their parents desperately tried to hide them from conscription. Mussi was not lucky enough to escape enlistment, and at a tender age found himself fighting in a war which he barely understood, the victim of someone else's brawl.

Yet Mussi had another challenge to face. As a member of the Beta Israel or Falasha community of Ethiopia, he was brought up as a Jew by his loving parents. This title turned out to be one of the hardest encumbrances to bear, for the general populace treated the "Falashas" with much scorn, and often with outright hatred. It was not uncommon for members of the community to be viciously beaten for having looked at a passing non-Jewish child with a "bad eye."

For six or seven years Mussi suffered in the army, facing situations which called on strengths well beyond his years. When he was close to 20 years of age, he made up his mind to escape. One night he slipped out of his camp and went AWOL. Mussi did not return home, but instead chose to flee to a faraway village, where he calculated the army would not find him. He settled there, changed his name, and always avoided questions regarding his past.

For eight or nine years, Mussi remained in the village, carefully guarding his secret, perpetually fearful of being discovered. It was in this village that he felt an indescribable revival of his Jewish identity, and from his earliest days there, he longed to learn more about his heritage. One day, Mussi came into possession of a small portable radio. At first he thought it would only offer him entertainment. Then, as he fiddled with the tuning knob one night, browsing through the various stations in his native Amharic language, he heard a strange tongue emanate from the speaker. He understood none of the individual words, and it was only when he heard the word "Tel Aviv" that he realized what he had discovered. It was a long-range broadcast from Israel.

From that day onwards, Mussi was possessed by a powerful drive to learn the Hebrew language. During the daytime, he worked hard to support himself, but when night fell and silence descended over the village, Mussi would glue himself to his trusty receiver, drinking in every word, for many hours into the night. An uncle of his who had made it to the Holy Land once returned to Ethiopia to visit the family, and left Mussi a simple Hebrew-Amharic dictionary containing a few hundred basic words. This dictionary, together with the radio, became his most prized possessions.

The dictionary was not the only treasure Mussi received from his uncle. Together with it he received a pair of *tefillin* and a *tallis*, items which were virtually unheard of in Ethiopia. Every day, Mussi would lovingly wrap himself in the *tallis* and place the *tefillin* carefully on his arm and head. Then he would pray from his *siddur*, a *siddur* that he had obtained in Ethiopia which contained the prayers in the Amharic language.

Life in the village was lonely, but at least he felt that he was progressing in some way. Within a short while, Mussi was understanding almost everything the radio reporters in faraway Israel were saying. Then one night, Mussi's whole world came tumbling down.

Someone rushed into his hut with an urgent message. It was a tip-off. The police were coming for him. The army did not take well to abandonment, and Mussi knew of the dire punishment he would face if he was taken. Without hesitation, he carefully packed his *tefillin, tallis,* and *siddur* into a small bag, and two suits and a few changes of clothes. He took a secret stash of money which he had been saving for just such an occasion and tucked it deftly into a small pocket inside his belt. Then he slipped silently into the night. It was the beginning of a long and incredible journey.

Now that there was a price on his head, Mussi knew that he had to leave the country. That night he caught a bus going south, toward the Kenyan border. A few kilometers before the border town of Moyale, he alighted and set out on foot. He walked fast, leaving the road behind him and making a wide berth around the town and the border post. He walked through the night, and in the early hours of the morning he slipped through the fence into Kenya. By the time he reached a road, he had been walking for many hours and had covered many kilometers. He flagged down a passing car and paid the man to take him on southwards, past the towering Mount Kenya, to the bustling city of Nairobi.

Mussi spent three weeks in Nairobi, relishing the intoxicating feeling of freedom and absorbing the sights and sounds of a new country. Despite the freedom, however, he still felt apprehensive regarding his safety and it was because of this that he left the city, once again traveling in a southerly direction, toward the Tanzanian border. Twenty kilometers before the border, he disembarked from the taxi he had hired, and once again he set out on foot into the bush. After bypassing the border, he slipped through the fence into Tanzania. When he eventually came to a road, he caught a bus to the Tanzanian city of Arusha and from there to the capital, the coastal city of Dar Es Salaam.

It was a Friday when he arrived in the capital, and he decided to check into a small hotel for Shabbos. It was there that he overheard two fellow Ethiopians discussing the merits of various African destinations, and it was from them that he first heard of the great opportunities available in South Africa, and specifically in its largest city, Johannesburg. By Saturday night, Mussi had made up his mind: He was going to Johannesburg, and nothing was going to stop him.

From Dar Es Salaam there are two options available for a traveler with little money wishing to journey southwards. The first is the sea route, a far more comfortable and direct option, but one which Mussi was understandably apprehensive about, considering that he was traveling without any documents or passports. Thus he chose the second option, the long and arduous land route, which, according to the people that he asked, would take him through the countries of Malawi, Mozambique, Swaziland, and finally South Africa.

The next morning he set out from Dar Es Salaam towards the Malawi border. As had become his custom, he let himself off the bus in the early afternoon some thirty kilometers before the border, and began hiking through the bush. He walked for some three and a half hours, looking up only to set his course. It thus came as a surprise to him when he suddenly realized that the light was fading. For a moment he was gripped with fear as the realization dawned on him that he would be spending the night in the bush somewhere in the middle of a strange African country. He quickly brought his fear under control, and called on all the years he had spent developing faith and *emunah* in Hashem to carry himself forward. He walked for a few more minutes, and then, in the murky half-light of dusk, hoisted himself up into the branches of a large tree.

Mussi removed his shoes, and hung them alongside his bag in the lower branches of the tree. He climbed a little higher and found a comfortable-looking crook between a branch and the trunk into which he squeezed his small frame. He then prepared himself to face the long night ahead.

Needless to say, sleep did not come easily. Around the tree, the bush began to rouse itself with the sounds of millions of creatures preparing to spend the night hunting or being hunted. Mussi dozed.

It was somewhere around 10 o' clock. Mussi woke up to an un-usual sound coming from beneath his tree. He rubbed his eyes and peered into the darkness, trying to make out the source of the sound. A wave of terror suddenly coursed through his body. A large pair of eyes were peering up at him from the ground directly below the tree. Around the eyes he could faintly make out the flow-ing mane of a huge male lion. As his eyes adjusted to the darkness he made out another and another. After a few minutes he counted a total of ten lions, an entire pride, clustered around his tree.

The lions seemed quite curious at first, pacing around the tree and peering into its branches with their large glowing eyes. After a few minutes of deliberation, they appeared to lose interest. However, just as Mussi's heart rate began to subside, one of the large males casually lay down alongside the tree trunk. As if on cue, the entire pride followed suit. Mussi clung to the tree, once again gripped by fear.

The fear did not last long. After a short while, Mussi once again summoned up his courage and began to pray. He opened his *sid-dur* and began to recite various psalms in his native Amharic. After a while he reached Psalm 91, the chapter which describes the confidence one can have in Hashem in times of difficulties: "He will charge His angels to protect you on all your travels. On palms they will carry you, lest you strike your foot against a stone. Upon the lion and the viper you will tread; you will tram-ple the young lion and the serpent."

As Mussi read these words, he was filled with confidence and faith. He pictured his bag hanging between him and the li-ons, and he told himself that the *tefillin* in it were like the *mezuzah* on the doorpost of a house, protecting its residents from any harm. He recited Psalm 91 many more times through-out the night.

At about 4 o'clock in the morning Mussi heard rustling below, and minutes later the lions had all padded silently away. Mussi recited *Modeh Ani* with fervent concentration, and when the sun crept over the horizon a few minutes later, there was not a single sign of his unusual late-night visitors.

For another three hours, Mussi remained in the tree, concerned that the lions were still in the close vicinity. At about 7 in the morning, he lowered his aching body to the ground and warily placed his shoes on his feet. He set out once again in the direction of the border. After twenty minutes of hard walking, he came to a wide river. Ignoring the possibility of crocodiles, he placed his bag on his head and swam across. He had arrived in Malawi.

After a further hour's walk, he came to a road. He flagged down the first car that rattled by, and paid the driver to take him to the nearest village, which was called Karonga, on the northern shores of Lake Nyasa. From there he traveled south, stopping in Mzuzu before reaching the Malawian capital, Lilongwe.

After a night in Lilongwe, he again headed south toward the nearby Mozambican border. Once again he bypassed the border, successfully crossing into northwestern Mozambique. A passing van picked him up near the border and gave him a lift to the nearest town, Tete, on the famous Zambezi River. From there he took five bus rides down the length of Mozambique, each bus carrying its passengers to the bank of a swollen river, at which the passengers would disembark and ford the rushing waters on their own. Another bus would be waiting on the far bank to take them further, until they reached the next river.

When he finally reached the capital Maputo, Mussi used his dwindling money to purchase 400 rands in South African currency which he stashed in his shoe. He replaced what remained of the $1200 he had started out with in the secret compartment in his belt. From Maputo he again traveled southwest toward the town of Namaacha on the Swaziland border. On board the bus, he asked the driver where the border lay and how to cross it. The man pointed to a prominent hill on the horizon and described how to find the fence from there. Mussi alighted and headed for the hill. After some hiking, he came to a fence. A few minutes of careful examination of the wires revealed a small hole, which he casually slipped through. Thus Mussi Dawa entered Swaziland.

From the border, Mussi trekked a further twenty-five kilometers through heavy bush until he came to a road. There he waited a few hours before successfully flagging down a passing motorist who agreed to give him a ride to the Swazi city of Manzini. From there he caught a taxi in the direction of South Africa, once again alighting a short distance from the border. On the instruction of the taxi driver, Mussi set out along a well-worn path which wound its way toward the fence between the two countries.

After walking for some thirty minutes, Mussi was surprised to hear someone calling out to him. He turned to see six menacing-looking men approaching him. "Wait, wait!" they shouted. For a moment he considered running, but he knew that he would not get far. He was in unfamiliar territory and his body was tired and weak from his strenuous travels. The men covered the one hundred meters between them slowly, appearing quite confident. As they approached, Mussi noticed how three of them wore nothing but trousers and shoes, their upper bodies glistening in the heat and covered with numerous tattoos.

"Hey, hey," said one of them. "Where you going, mister?" It was only then that Mussi noticed the knife clenched in the man's hand. Its glistening blade was enough to convince him to cooperate. "Johannesburg," he replied in his steadiest voice. "What for?" inquired the knife-wielding hoodlum. "To live," answered Mussi, desperately trying not to show his fear. He had come so far to reach this point, and was determined not to let these ruffians stop him.

"You got any money?" the man asked gruffly, and then as if to explain himself, added: "We need money." Mussi remained silent. Two of the men then approached him and began to search him. After a few moments, their experienced hands discovered the rands in his shoe, which they hastily stuffed into their pockets. Fortunately for Mussi, however, they did not find his secret compartment in the back of his belt where his dollars were stashed. Having finished searching his person, the men then turned to the small bag Mussi had with him.

One of the men kneeled on the floor and pulled items of clothing out of the bag. Presently, a grunt attracted the attention of his henchmen, who clustered around to see what he had uncovered.

Mussi felt a sudden wave of anger rush through him. They had found his *tefillin* bag. The men pushed Mussi closer to the knapsack and then, poking the velvet *tefillin* bag gingerly, asked Mussi what it contained. "*Tefillin*," replied Mussi defiantly. "Not money?" asked the thug. "No," replied Mussi. Then as an afterthought, Mussi added menacingly: "If you touch them you will die."

The men hesitated for a moment and then began conversing among themselves in a language Mussi did not understand. Then, to his amazement, they stepped back from his bag as if afraid of something. "Put it away," they commanded, pointing at the *tefillin* bag cautiously. Mussi stuffed it into his knapsack.

Realizing that he was in a strong position, Mussi told the men that they had taken all the money that he owned, and that he would be unable to proceed on his journey if they did not return it. The man who had taken his cash hesitated for a moment, and then carefully drew a few bills from his pocket, which he handed to Mussi. Mussi then asked them to direct him toward the border, which they did. Then, as suddenly as they had appeared, the men were gone.

After a few kilometers of walking, Mussi once again came to a fence. However, unlike all the other ones that he had crossed on his epic journey, this one was electrified. Unsure of what to do, he began to walk along a well-worn path which ran parallel to the fence. He studied the fence carefully, trying to work out how to penetrate its menacing wires. Presently, he came to large tree which was rooted on the Swaziland side of the border, but whose branches towered high above the fence and into South African territory. The day was waning and there was little time for deliberation. As a child, Mussi had been an expert tree climber, and for the first time in his life, the skill was going to prove its true value. Mussi hoisted himself into the tree and began to clamber up through its branches. He found a sturdy-looking branch, and slowly edged along the branch until he was safely over the fence. He then peered down cautiously to assess his altitude. He was a few meters above the ground, but he knew that it was his only chance. He dropped his bag to the ground. Now he was committed. He closed his eyes for a moment and then cast himself bravely into the abyss. The ground came up at him with a vengeance and he felt his leg twisting as he crumpled into a heap on the South African side of the border. Mussi had arrived.

After a few minutes of recovery time, Mussi raised himself to his feet and began hobbling away from the fence. For a couple of hours he walked until he came across a sandy road. Minutes after he found the road, a small pickup truck came thundering along in a cloud of dust. In the driver's seat was a large Afrikaans man, who stopped quickly on seeing Mussi on the roadside. The passenger door opened, and Mussi collapsed onto the seat, almost too exhausted to speak. As the man set out along the road, Mussi dredged up the strength tell the man his story. He told him of the army and his escape from Ethiopia; he told him of the many countries he had past through and of his dream of reaching Johannesburg. He described to the man his frightening rendezvous with the thugs on the Swazi side of the border and how they had stolen much of his money. Finally he told him of his terrifying leap from the giant tree into South Africa. The man was spellbound.

After a 90-kilometer drive, they pulled into a small town. The man took Mussi into the general store on the main road. There, he bought Mussi some food and a cold drink, and while Mussi sat outside satisfying his ravenous hunger, the man disappeared into the store a second time. Minutes later he appeared outside with a parcel. In it Mussi found two pairs of trousers, a shirt, and some underclothes.

Mussi thanked the man profusely, and then asked him how he could get to Johannesburg. The man carefully drew him a map, before stopping a passing car, the driver of which agreed to take him to Johannesburg. As Mussi climbed into the vehicle, his benefactor, the man who he knew simply as "David," pressed a 100-rand note into his hand. Then he was gone.

Walking down a road in the Johannesburg suburb of Berea a few weeks later, Mussi was overjoyed to see a beautiful shul on the opposite side of the road. After a short and humorous negotiation with the security guard who had never seen a Jew with dark skin before, Mussi was eventually admitted into the shul whose rabbi welcomed him warmly. Since that day, Mussi has found a place for himself in the Johannesburg Jewish community. He recently completed a full proper conversion (as has become customary among the Jews of Ethiopia whose Jewish lineage is not as clearly defined as other Jewish groups), and is today a religious and committed Jew.

At the conclusion of my interview I asked Mussi, who today goes by the name Eliezer, if he has traveled to Israel since his arrival in South Africa. He studied me for a moment, and then, with a twinkle in his eyes, replied: "Yes, in my dreams."

In a short while, Eliezer's dream will come true. He has been accepted into a yeshivah in Israel and hopes to make *aliyah* within a few months. When he does, it will be the final leg of a most inspiring journey, a journey which took him through some 4000 kilometers of hostile African landscape and through six international borders. His frightening encounter with the lions, as well as his ironic incident with the Swazi thugs who eventually showed him the way to the border, will remain with him forever, as will the memory of his improbable benefactor who helped him get to Johannesburg where he was able to reunite with his Jewish roots. Indeed, it has been a remarkable journey, in both the physical and spiritual senses of the word.

▪ Long Walk to Freedom

We all face challenges in our lives: the proverbial mountains we must climb, difficult paths we must trudge, and terrifying chasms we must traverse. At times we feel that these challenges are bigger than us, that we are not "cut out" for the lives we are meant to lead. It is at times like these that we must remember that the challenges and trials we face are tailor made by the Director of all existence. Our experiences unite to form the tapestry of our lives.

The commentators note that the Hebrew word for "trial" or "challenge" is essentially identical to the Hebrew word which means "flagpole." They explain that just as the purpose of a flagpole is to raise up the essential character of a country, the flag, for all to see, so too the purpose of a trial or challenge is to raise up and demonstrate the essential character of a person.

On a cold motza'ei Shabbos *not long ago, I sat around a table with a remarkable family who told me their harrowing story. It is a story of terrifying challenge, yet it is a story of the power of the human spirit to overcome even the most daunting of trials. It is a story which proves that the challenges we face are personalized, perfectly suited for our innate strengths. In many ways, it is the story of a remarkable journey, the figurative road that every one of us has the ability to traverse.*

The Kruger National Park is a vast and unspoiled tract of wilderness situated in the northeastern corner of South Africa. It is bordered on the east by Mozambique, on the west by a man-made boundary, and on the north and south by the Limpopo and Crocodile rivers, respectively. The scale of the park is barely comprehensible. It stretches some three hundred and fifty kilometers from south to north, and occupies just less than two million hectares of land, making it approximately the same size as the entire State of Israel. Nearly three thousand kilometers of road wind their way through the wilderness, punctuated inter-mittently by rest camps and picnic spots. In the main part, however, the park is nothing but unspoiled wilderness, where the mark of human civilization can at times be entirely forgotten. This makes it one of the prime tourist attractions in South Africa, and every day, more than three thousand people pass through its gates. Once inside they will spend the day edging their way through the bush, eyes peering eagerly through the windows of their cars as they long for a glimpse of one of the park's mammalian, avian, or reptilian residents. Chances are that they will be rewarded, too, for the park contains a rich diversity of animal life. The numbers are remarkable here as well: 147 species of mammal and 114 species of reptile roam freely within its confines. Over 8,000 elephants have been counted, as well as nearly 15,000 buffalo and some 3,000 rhinoceros. The remaining two species which make up the "Big Five" are also abundant, with regular sightings of lions and leopards in all parts of the park.

For the human visitors, however, the park is only for daytime pleasure. As the reddish sun begins to descend towards the horizon, the cars begin to slink one by one into the security of the fenced-in rest camps or toward the nearest exit gate. Within a few minutes of sunset, the gates are closed and locked, and as darkness cloaks the bushveld, the park becomes the domain of the prowling animals.

Rabbi Avraham Ehrman lives with his family in the northern suburbs of Johannesburg, where he is a rebbi in one of the religious day schools in the area. Originally from Israel, the family arrived in South Africa a few years ago and soon became valued members of the close-knit community.

In September 2000, Rabbi Ehrman's son Dovid, who had been studying in Israel, visited South Africa to spend the High Holidays and Succos with his family. After celebrating *Yom Tov* together, the family decided that a vacation was in order, and elected to spend a few days with some friends in the resort town of Sabie in the Mpumalanga province. They invited another family to join them, and immediately after Succos the Ehrmans and Rubatzis set out for the small town.

The first two days in Sabie passed peacefully, and the Ehrman and Rubatzi families were preparing to spend their third and final day there, when Dovid suggested that they spend it instead in the Kruger National Park. He had heard so much about the park, and was very eager to see it firsthand. Thus at about midday on the Wednesday after Succos, the two families entered the Kruger, intending to tour until the gates closed. The cars were already packed with all their luggage and the plan was to drive on to Johannesburg immediately after exiting the park.

They headed into the park in close formation, but after a short while, the car at the rear, belonging to the Ehrmans, slowed down in order to widen the gap between them and the lead car. The road which they were traveling on was made of loose sand, and the dust from the lead car was spoiling their vision. In this way they traveled most of the afternoon, studying the remarkable flora and fauna found in the southern parts of the park. By 5 o'clock in the afternoon, the gap between the cars was quite sizable, which did not concern Rabbi Ehrman unduly because he had arranged to meet up with the other vehicle at the Malelane exit gate, where they intended to *daven Minchah* together before setting out for Johannesburg.

On the back seat of the Ehrmans' car was the rabbi himself as well as his daughters, Menuchah and Efrat. Dovid was at the wheel, with Chananel by his side in the front passenger seat. Mrs. Ehrman had opted to travel with the Rubatzis in the other car.

At about 5:30, they suddenly felt the car vibrating dramatically, and as Rabbi Ehrman raised his voice to instruct him to stop the vehicle, Dovid lost control. The car swerved violently, before turning onto its side. They scraped harshly along the gravel road for some twenty meters before the car once again spun around and came to a rest on its roof. For a moment, silence reigned, then bedlam erupted.

Rabbi Ehrman called from the back to ask whether everyone was all right. His call was echoed by a similar one from Dovid, who passed out moments later. As the dust settled, Chananel pulled himself free of the car, and was soon followed by his father. Together they helped Efrat out from the back seat; she appeared to be relatively unscathed. In the front seat, Dovid was completely unresponsive, and as they pulled him from the car, Rabbi Ehrman found himself thinking the worst. They shook him gently and poured water on his face. After a few minutes they noticed his fingers moving and a short while later he began to come around. A trickle of blood ran down his face from a gash on his head.

Last out of the car was Menuchah, who appeared at the time to be only slightly hurt, her hair masking the wound she had received on her scalp. At first, Dovid was highly disoriented, demanding to know where he was and how the car had come to be in such a state. After a few minutes, however, he began to come to his senses. With some clothing removed from inside the upturned car, Rabbi Ehrman bandaged Dovid's head and then, noticing Menuchah's wound for the first time, bandaged her as well. Only then did he stop to take stock of their situation.

The map they had purchased earlier in the day was lost somewhere in the wreck of their car. However, due to a remarkable piece of *hashgachah pratis*, Rabbi Ehrman had studied it thoroughly moments before the accident, noting their exact location and the distance between them and the exit gate. The situation looked bleak. In a few short minutes, the gates would be closing. No human being would pass their way until morning. The only mobile phone was in the other car. The sun was setting, and on the other horizon, storm clouds gathered.

It did not take long for Rabbi Ehrman to make a decision. He *davened* a heartfelt *Minchah*, raising his voice in a plaintive cry during the prayer for health and healing. Then, he informed the children that they were going to walk to safety. He did not tell them that it lay some sixteen kilometers away, nor did he remind them of the fact that they were deep in the heart of "Big Five" territory.

At about 6:30 they set out, carrying some fruit they had found in the car, a bottle of water, and some matches. At first, both Menuchah and Dovid needed to be supported, but later, Dovid felt his strength returning and was able to walk unassisted. With the distant rumble of thunder in the background, the battered family trudged toward the Malelane gate. Every few minutes, Menuchah would complain that she needed to stop, begging them to let her sleep. Rabbi Ehrman knew that it could be a fatal mistake to allow her to sleep even for a minute, and he insisted that she stay on her feet when they stopped to rest. Progress was slow, and as they walked they peered nervously into the bushes, expecting a large beast to emerge at every turn.

At one point, Dovid thought he saw a pair of eyes glowing in the darkness alongside the road and they quickened their pace at the thought. Later, they heard roaring in the distance, which the children thought might be a helicopter coming to their rescue. Rabbi Ehrman knew otherwise. Not long before the accident, they had seen a large lion alongside the road.

After a while, Rabbi Ehrman decided that it was necessary to raise the family's flagging spirits, and to try to distract them from thinking about what they were doing. Rabbi Ehrman had been a *chazan* for many years, and he began to sing the Yom Kippur service. With lightning flickering in the distance, his children sang along with him. Later, when they had run out of songs, he began to tell them stories, inspiring them to go on, and distracting them from their pain and surroundings. At one point during the walk, their courageous father encouraged the children to accept upon themselves to do something extra as a source of merit, an act of charity, or some other *mitzvah* to perform when they returned home. Little by little he coaxed them onwards, toward the gate and safety.

Rabbi Ehrman was relatively confident about their route, but nevertheless chose to stop at each crossroad and study the signposts carefully by the light of a match. After some three hours of walking, they saw the distant lights of the highway and close to an hour later, they arrived at the inner gate of the park. (The park has two gates, an outer one which is locked to keep the public out at night, and an inner one, which is not locked, to keep the animals inside. Between the two gates are a number of offices and administration buildings.)

Alongside one of the buildings, Rabbi Ehrman found a public telephone from where he placed a call to a toll-free emergency number. He described the situation to the dispatcher who promised to send an ambulance immediately. Then, she patched him through to the mobile phone in the Rubatzis' car.

While the group had been walking, Mrs. Ehrman and the Rubatzis had been beside themselves with worry. Half an hour after the gates closed, they realized that something must have happened to the other vehicle, and begged the guard at the gate to let them in once again. He refused, and would not even listen to their pleas, as he had strict instructions not to let anyone into the park after sunset, and appeared not to understand English. After a half hour of frustration and anxiety, they decided to look for help elsewhere. They did not find any, and it was the ring of the mobile phone which finally relieved them of their misery.

It was close to 11 o'clock that night when the ambulance pulled up to the front gate of the park. The flashing lights and shrieking siren were enough to bring the guard to his senses, and he quickly opened the gate and let the emergency vehicle through. The attendants applied proper dressings to Dovid and Menuchah's head wounds before loading them into the ambulance and rushing them to a nearby hospital in the town of Malelane. The small-town hospital was not equipped to deal with their injuries, and they were once again placed in the ambulance and rushed to a larger town in the area called Nelspruit. From there they hoped to be evacuated by airplane to an adequate facility in Johannesburg.

The storm which had been brewing the entire evening finally broke, and on their arrival in Nelspruit, word arrived from Johannesburg that the plane could not take off due to the storm which was also raging there. It was only the following afternoon that they set out by ambulance from the Nelspruit hospital for Johannesburg, arriving at the Linksfield clinic four hours later, some twenty-two hours after their accident.

The clinic was expecting them, and both Menuchah and Dovid were wheeled straight into surgery. Both had suffered significant head wounds, although brain scans showed that there was no brain damage. Within a week they were both on the road to recovery and were discharged from the clinic.

The Ehrman family had their moment of fame, too. Stories appeared in two major Johannesburg papers describing the family's remarkable experience in the wilderness. It had been a harrowing test of the family's resolve, but their simple faith and piety had carried them through. Indeed, the challenge seems to have strengthened them as a family, and raised them up high for all to see the power of hard-earned *emunah*.

Our Sages tell us that the shofar blown at Sinai as the backdrop to the giving of the Torah was not the horn of an ordinary ram. That shofar, we are told, was made from the left horn of the ram which Avraham had slaughtered in place of his son Yitzchak at the *Akeidah*. Interestingly, with reference to the shofar which will be blown to herald the arrival of *Mashiach*, *Chazal* tell us that it will be fashioned from the right horn of that very same ram. There is a difference between them, however, for the shofar reserved for Messianic times is referred to as "a great shofar," while at Sinai it was but an ordinary one. What is meant by these cryptic statements of the Sages?

The ram that Avraham sacrificed on that fateful day was a substitute for his son. Hashem had tested Avraham's commitment to Him in a most terrifying way, and the founder of our nation had stood up to the test. It was the energy created by that self-sacrifice, represented by the sound of the shofar, which allowed his descendants to receive the Torah at Sinai.

In the time of *Mashiach*, that energy will be added to all the energy created by the self-sacrifice of the millions of Jews who have lived since then, and who have suffered and given their lives to observe Hashem's will. All of that cumulative self-sacrifice will rise up in the crescendo of the "great shofar" that will herald *Mashiach's* arrival.

(As heard in a *shiur* by Rav Aharon Pfeuffer, *zt"l*)

Every single day, thousands of Jews make sacrifices to maintain their unswerving loyalty to Hashem. It is a characteristic which has preserved us through the generations, has earned us the title of "the chosen people," and is a characteristic which will eventually merit us to see the coming of *Mashiach*, speedily in our days.

▪ Shema Yisrael

There is an age-old custom for a child begining to learn Chumash *for the first time in his life to be taught the Book of* Vayikra. *This volume deals predominantly with the laws of the* Kohanim *in the Holy Temple, the sacrifices, and the maintenance of true spiritual purity.* Chazal *explain this custom using the expression, "Let the pure ones come and involve themselves in matters of purity."*

*We are also taught, "The world is sustained only as a result of the breaths of the mouths of the children in their places of learning" (*Shabbos 119*).*

It is clear from these sources that there exists in children a certain element of purity and truthfulness which is not to be found in adults. Life is indeed simple, but as we grow up we make it complicated for ourselves. Children see the world through very honest eyes.

This was brought home to me in a very powerful manner one evening a few years ago.

It was just after sunset, that time zone when it is neither dark enough for headlights nor light enough to go without. I found myself in a neighborhood through which I seldom travel at that time of day, having been taken out of my way by a student who needed a ride home after school. After dropping him off, I was making my way back to my side of town when I approached an intersection. As I cruised toward the traffic light, I noticed that it had just turned yellow, and for a moment I hesitated as to whether to take the prudent approach and stop a few seconds early, or zip through the intersection. At the last minute I chose the former option and brought my car to a halt behind the white line.

As I sat at the intersection after a long day of teaching, I watched through the windshield as cars crisscrossed in front of me, left to right and right to left, taking advantage of the green traffic light favoring them. Through my weariness and the twilight gloom I could vaguely make out some pedestrians on the far side of the intersection waiting patiently to cross toward me. Suddenly, out of the corner of my eye I noticed some rapid movement to my left. I swung my head around to identify the figure, and watched as a small boy wearing a yarmulka carelessly raced toward the intersection, his mind lost in some boyish adventure or fantasy.

As he skipped exuberantly down the sidewalk, he glanced up briefly to make sure that the traffic light was still green. Seeing that indeed it was, he ran in front of my stationary car, almost without slowing. Suddenly I felt my stomach lurch. A large car was turning across the intersection, and to my horror I realized that its path would directly intersect that of the prancing child.

My brain screamed instructions to every part of me, but that split second from when I noticed what was happening until it happened was not long enough, and instead every muscle in my body tensed and waited for the impact. When it came, it was not quite what I had braced myself for. The car had reached the point of impact milliseconds before the child, so the boy effectively collided with the car rather than the other way around. My mortified limbs finally came to life and I leapt from my car to assess the damage.

I found the child lying alongside the car, his face twisted in pain, sobbing, "My leg, my leg." To my horror I noticed that his leg appeared to be pinned beneath the front wheel of the vehicle.

The woman who had been driving the car began to climb out, screaming hysterically as she did. A passerby also began to howl, and for a few moments pandemonium reigned.

I realized that the first priority was to free the child's leg, which seemed to be trapped at the ankle beneath the tire. In my sternest voice, I instructed the woman to get into her car and slowly back up.

It took her a few precious moments to react, but she finally climbed into the car and backed it slowly away. I crouched down by the child's side while dialing for help on my mobile phone.

Having done all that I could, I turned my attention to the small figure sprawled on the hard road in the darkening gloom. He was lying on his back, clutching his left leg, sobbing. I took his hand and tried to mask the shakiness in my own voice as I told him that help was on the way. "Everything's going to be okay," I said hesitantly. Suddenly he began to blurt out what sounded like a Hebrew phrase. It was only when he repeated it a second and third time that I absorbed what he was saying, and an icy chill ran up my spine.

"Shema Yisrael Hashem Elokeinu Hashem Echad."

He sobbed briefly, and then again repeated,

"Shema Yisrael Hashem Elokeinu Hashem Echad. Shema Yisrael Hashem Elokeinu Hashem Echad."

I clutched his hand tighter and leaned closer to him. "You're going to be all right, little fellow," I said urgently. It was too much for me to hear this little child reciting the *Shema,* the verse a dying man says before he leaves this world. I almost began to plead with him, to tell him that the *Shema* was not necessary, but I stopped myself. To discuss the appropriateness of the *Shema* would have been to confront the possibility of death, which seemed ridiculous at the time. "It's just your leg," was all I could muster, "and there's help on the way, my brave little friend."

He appeared not to have heard me and once again he blurted out:

"Shema Yisrael Hashem Elokeinu Hashem Echad."

A doctor who was driving past rushed over to us and crouched alongside the child's injured leg. After a cursory examination of the limb, he gently pried the boy's shoe off and flexed his ankle tenderly. After a minute of further examination it became apparent that, miraculously, the boy had no broken bones, and had suffered only some serious grazing and bruises. By the time a Hatzalah volunteer roared up to the intersection, the child had already been hoisted into someone's arms and was being carried toward the sidewalk, away from the intersecion.

As I digested the event over the next few days, I came to the conclusion that I had been "set up," that I had almost been manipulated to ensure that I got a front-row seat to the whole incredible incident. It was clear to me that it was a "setup," for I seldom if ever find myself on that side of town in the early evening. Furthermore, I had been delayed by a few minutes even before I left the school to take my student home. And those minutes counted. But even the seconds counted, the seconds leading up to the yellow traffic light. And the split-second decision not to rush through the traffic light, which ensured that I was sitting at exactly the right spot, to watch the entire incident unfold before my eyes.

And when I analyzed the accident itself through those same eyes, I was suddenly overwhelmed by the precise coordination of its every facet.

The little boy was only in that spot because he was running at a moderate pace. Had he taken his steps just a little faster, he would most certainly have been directly in the path of the huge vehicle.

And had he delayed, or run slightly slower, not only would he not have been struck at all, but not a single person on this planet would have even been aware of what might have happened at that intersection on that gloomy Monday evening.

And had the driver of the big car not dropped her keys as she was leaving her home, or had she not slowed for another vehicle along the way, she would most certainly have arrived at the intersection a second or two earlier, with frightening repercussions. And had she been delayed by a few seconds more, once again the world would have been blissfully unaware of the little boy and what might have happened to his leg.

One cannot live one's life trying to predict the long-term ramifications of every tiny move and decision that we make. Such an attempt would surely lead to madness. But it is critical that we realize that there is a Coordinator, a Director. Life is made up not of a series of "what might have happened's" but rather by a perfect fusion of the things that do indeed happen.

And having thought about it, I decided that the little boy was not wrong in the way he reacted to what had happened to him.

Indeed, he was 100 percent correct. *Shema Yisrael, Hashem Elokeinu, Hashem Echad.*

▪ Du Bist a Yid?

Hashgachah pratis means that the effects of a particular event, whether good or bad, are measured and weighed to ensure that they precisely match the requirements of every person involved.

My teacher, Rav Aharon Pfeuffer, zt"l, once quoted the following story in a shiur. I subsequently heard it again from one of the parties. He explained that no single act, no matter how small it may be, goes unnoticed. Every deed and action has a consequence, and in the end the right people are brought together.

By the beginning of the 1930's, Henry Posen considered himself an accomplished man. Since his birth in 1896 in the German city of Frankfurt-am-Main, success had never eluded him, and it was there that he married his wife, started a family, and established a successful banking business. He traveled frequently, developing useful contacts in many European cities, and through them becoming familiar with the idiosyncrasies of each country's financial establishments. There was little a man in his position had to worry about — if not for the Nazis, that is. By 1933, Henry sensed that the heavy black clouds gathering over Germany were not going to disperse placidly, and he began restructuring his financial affairs. In 1936 he commenced a systematic downsizing of his banking interests in Germany and shortly afterwards he established a branch in Belgium to take their place. On October 25, 1938, Henry and his family left Germany for England. They were among the tiny minority who managed to escape before the storm broke and obliterated Western Europe and its Jewish inhabitants.

Four years prior to his immigration to England, while on a trip to Paris, Henry had met a cousin who resided in France at the time. This cousin approached Henry for assistance in transferring certain funds out of Germany to be sent to England. Henry agreed to help and a short while after his return to Germany, Henry had set about transferring the money. The elaborate scheme he chose to use was one which he had used successfully before. This involved delivering the money to a Jewish cook aboard an American ship berthed in the Frankfurt harbor. The cook would then stash the money away somewhere on the ship and pass it on to a designated agent on arrival in England. Unfortunately, on the particular voyage that Henry chose to ferry his cousin's funds, the cook happened to be carrying money for numerous people and somewhere along the way, he was betrayed to the authorities. Before the ship set sail, a band of Gestapo agents raided the craft and discovered the large quantity of cash hidden in the heating pipes. The Gestapo confiscated all the money, and it was only thanks to the intervention of the American captain that the cook was saved from arrest. The entire sum belonging to Henry's cousin was lost, never to be recovered.

When Henry informed his cousin of what had happened, the man was incensed and accused him of embezzling the funds to line his own pocket. Henry vehemently denied these claims but to no avail. He began receiving threatening letters from the cousin who was still in Paris, letters which, if discovered by the authorities, could easily have endangered Henry's life, considering the political climate in Germany at the time.

On his arrival in London in 1938, Henry was confronted by another cousin, who also accused him of stealing the money. Again, Henry asserted that he had had no involvement in the loss of the money and had carried out his duties without failure.

Shortly after the war broke out, Henry received a telephone call from this cousin, again demanding compensation. When Henry again stated he did not owe the man any money, the man replied, "There are ways and means to force you to pay."

Not long after the telephone call, Henry received a summons to appear before a tribunal of the London Regional Alien Advisory

Committee, chaired by Sir Roland Burrows. Burrows was a notorious anti-Semite about whom, in Henry's words, "one could say nothing good." At his first appearance before the tribunal, Burrows grilled Henry as to what had happened to the money. He produced a letter Henry had written to his Parisian cousin while still in Germany, in which Henry had instructed his cousin not to send any further threatening letters which might endanger his life. This letter seemed to convince the judge of Henry's guilt. At no stage was he given a chance to defend himself, and he was finally instructed to repay his cousin the entire sum. Henry refused.

After his first appearance at the tribunal, Henry was allowed to return home. A second hearing was convened, followed by a third. At no stage was Henry allowed to come with a lawyer. At the third hearing, Burrows badgered Henry with hateful questions, wanting to know why his German passport was not stamped "J" to indicate his being Jewish and why he had chosen to leave Germany. Finally, he demanded to know whether Henry possessed any money in England. When he responded in the affirmative, Burrows wanted to know whether he was aware that it was illegal for a German citizen to possess money outside of its borders. When he conceded that he was aware of such legislation, Burrows pounced: "So you were disloyal to your country, I see," he spat. "Now, of what use do you think your presence is in this country?" The trial was effectively over. Burrows informed Henry that he would be interned for the duration of the war as a German, together with his wife and children. Henry was termed a category "A" prisoner, the worst possible classification, while his wife was given a "B" categorization. Their incarceration began in January 1940.

Henry began his internment in Chelsea, while his wife was sent to the Isle of Man together with their four children, aged 3 to 11. In Chelsea, Henry was placed together with a group of German "nobles": One introduced himself as "Von Richtofen," while another claimed to be related to Himmler. After several days, they were transferred to Seaton, a vacation resort on the coast of Devon, where the internees were allocated tents to keep out the winter cold. The camp was inhabited by a motley group including Nazis, non-Nazis, and a few Jews. At first, the English did not differentiate between Nazi and non-Nazi, blind to the irony of that state of affairs. Only later were the two groups separated. Some of the Nazi prisoners were subsequently released and were repatriated via Holland to Germany. Many of the Germans carefully avoided contact with the Jews. For a short while the internees were allowed to receive parcels and to send letters out once a week. Beginning in May 1940, all mail and newspapers were banned, and radios were confiscated.

In June 1940, half of the internees were transported out of Seaton and two weeks later the remainder, including Henry, were loaded onto a special train headed for an unknown destination. Henry boarded the train with nothing but a small suitcase. Only when the train finally crawled into Liverpool did the 300 men aboard begin suspecting what was in store for them. At the Liverpool docks they were joined by hundreds of other internees and were ordered to board a large ship moored there. In total, over 2000 men were forced to board the Andora Star that day, including Jews, Germans, and many Italians. The ship was bound for Australia, and was severely overcrowded.

On the night of June 20, the Andora Star sailed out of Liverpool; on board were the 2000 inmates as well as an English military escort. Henry was allocated a first-class cabin to be shared with eight other men. One morning, about 6:30, Henry was outside his room, walking about. While outside, he observed the weather to be unusually calm. About half an hour after returning to his room, he heard a strange sound emanating from the aft end of the ship. The sound was not a dramatic one, and he was almost tempted to ignore it when he heard a man muttering over and over to himself, "Now it's happened." Somewhat mystified, Henry tried the light switch but to no avail. Dashing out of the cabin, he found the men on board remarkably calm. It was beginning to dawn on him that the cause of the unusual sound had been a dreaded German torpedo, and that it was likely to have caused more than just an unusual sound. Evidently, most of the passengers were ignorant of this fact.

Henry later described the ensuing drama in his diary:

"I ran to the steerage deck, then back to the cabin to grab some of my clothes. While doing so, my watch fell to the floor. I left it there and ran to the part of the ship that was high. (The engine room had been hit, and was sinking faster than the forward section of the craft.) The people fought for places on the lifeboats, but only a few of the small boats were seaworthy enough to use. I found a big plank, which I threw into the sea. I jumped in after it and held on tight. Once in the water I swallowed quantities of oil (which was leaking from the floundering ship). At a distance, I spotted a float, made of two barrels with a bench attached, bobbing in the water. I abandoned my plank and swam to the float. Six men and I succeeded in saving our lives by clinging to that float.

"We tried to row the float, but were thwarted by a strong current. In the end we just hung on and watched the sinking ship. By 7:25, one end of the ship was high out of the water, and then it was gone. The ship sank quickly. Some 1000 men went down with the Andora Star that morning, including many of the Jews and Italians. A large percentage of the Germans survived. Ironically, after the ship was torpedoed, the German marine captain who happened to be among the internees went to the bridge of the ship and died alongside the English captain.

"Most of the lifeboats were lost at sea. Nearly all the old people drowned; bodies were washed away by the waves. At noon, a plane flew over us, and three hours later we sighted a Canadian battleship. Within an hour, they were fishing survivors out of the water. Some of the people who were saved died on board due to exhaustion and injuries. Most of the survivors were naked. The crew members on board the battleship tried to help us as much as possible, but they could not do much as there was not enough place aboard the ship, nor sufficient food. I hardly had any clothing on and was covered in oil. I succeeded in getting one cooked potato to eat."

The Canadian battleship put the survivors off at Greenock, near Glasgow, capital of Scotland. There, the miserable and exhausted survivors were placed under heavily armed surveillance by a company of soldiers. Henry was dressed in nothing but a raincoat and a pair of overshoes supplied by the Canadians. The prisoners were taken from the docks to an abandoned factory, under the supervision of a helpless old major who could not decide anything on his own, and who was continuously telephoning London for instructions. Food supplies were nonexistent, and the major's incompetence only compounded the problem. The survivors were forbidden from contacting their families and it was only many days later that they were permitted to send a single postcard stating simply: "I am safe." Henry managed to speak privately with a Scottish clergyman who had come to deliver a sermon. He was able to convince the man to write a more detailed note to his family, still imprisoned on the Isle of Man.

Two days after their rescue, the men were transported to a tent camp in the mountains not far from Edinburgh. The weather was freezing, and most of the prisoners still had inadequate clothing. The English guards were exceptionally obnoxious, insulting the captives and calling them Nazis.

One night, as Henry paced around the perimeter of the camp, he noticed a guard standing with his back to the fence, his arms thrust deep into his pockets in an attempt to stay warm. Something about the guard caught his attention: it may have been the man's stance or even perhaps his profile. Henry hesitated for a second and then, throwing caution to the wind, whispered urgently to the guard: *"Du bist a Yid?* — You are a Jew?"

The guard hesitated for a moment, as if he was unsure whether to respond. Henry could see that he was somewhat shocked by the unsolicited inquiry. Slowly the guard turned around. Henry's heart was beating wildly.

"Yes, my brother," was the response.

A chill ran up Henry's spine. From the man's demeanor, however, he could see that there was no time for casual conversation. Before he could think of a suitable response, the guard suddenly thrust his hand through the fence. Henry felt a small item being pressed into his hand, a piece of chocolate. Then the guard was gone.

The next day the prisoners were once again transferred, to Liverpool, where they were placed on yet another ship bound for Australia. This time the ship survived the perilous trip, and it was there that Henry sat out the rest of the war years. He never saw the guard again.

■   ■   ■

Bernard Kay was born in Leeds, a large Jewish center, in the year 1917. He grew up there in what was effectively a ghetto, surrounded mainly by Jewish families with very little contact with the outside world. Some of his family had immigrated to South Africa in the late 1800's, and on a visit to the United Kingdom an uncle who lived in Johannesburg suggested that Bernard accompany him back there, where there was greater opportunity for aspiring young men. In 1939, Bernard was determined to get out of England and his family made preparations for him to join his uncle on the boat trip back to South Africa. For various reasons, Bernard was unable to obtain a passport at the time and the ship left Southampton docks without him. Shortly thereafter, the Second World War broke out and on January 8, 1940, Bernard was conscripted into the British army.

Unlikely as it may sound, the young Jewish man was assigned to the Royal Scots Regiment, with its headquarters in Edinburgh, Scotland. Bernard always marveled how a *Yid* from the Leylands, the ghetto of Leeds, ended up in such a prestigious regiment, with their ancient traditions and idiosyncrasies. His anecdotes of his experiences in the regiment always elicited a smile, especially his descriptions of the poor Jewish boy having to wear a kilt. Bernard seems to recall that there may have been another Jewish soldier in the Royal Scots, although the man certainly never admitted to being Jewish, and instead joined another denomination for spiritual devotion every Sunday. There were no facilities for a Jewish soldier and certainly no services to attend.

Bernard was always conscious of the workings of Divine Providence in his life, and after a relatively short period of time with the regiment, he volunteered for another post which ultimately took him to North Africa and the invasion of Italy. This move probably saved his life, because the Royal Scots Regiment was nearly decimated in the battles that followed.

Just prior to his transfer, however, Bernard was ordered to stand guard duty with the Royal Scots one cold evening somewhere in Northern Scotland. He was briefed by his sergeant, who informed him that a German warship had been torpedoed and that the surviving sailors had been picked up by an allied ship and brought to Scotland. He was to guard these men for the night; he was told that they were dangerous Nazis and that he was to have absolutely no contact with them.

Bernard's assignment was to guard the perimeter fence surrounding a tent camp not far from Edinburgh where the prisoners were being held. Under no circumstances, he was warned, should he speak to any of the prisoners. It was a cold evening and as he circled the perimeter fence, clothed in his thick trench coat, few thoughts crossed his mind other than keeping warm and ensuring that there were no escapes from the compound. It was therefore a startling moment when he heard someone from behind the fence call out to him. It was even more startling that the person called out to him, not in English, not in German, but in Yiddish. The man who was at the fence, had called out the very familiar phrase, *"Du bist a Yid? —* You are a Jew?"

Scared out of his wits, and with his strict instructions ringing in his ears, he approached a little closer and answered with a muffled, "Yes, my brother." The prisoner proceeded to ask whether he had anything to give him. Bernard felt in the pocket of his trench coat and found a piece of chocolate which he handed to the shivering man behind the fence. For the rest of that cold night, Bernard mulled over what had transpired in the short meeting, wondering to himself how a fellow Jew had ended up as a prisoner among the Nazis. By morning, he had made up his mind to take the risk of searching for the man when he came back on duty the following night, this time with more provisions in his pocket. That day the prisoners were transferred. Bernard never saw the man again.

After demobilization in 1947, Bernard came back from Italy to the United Kingdom and settled down with his wife from whom he had been separated — due to the war — since their marriage in 1941. They initially settled in Cardiff in Wales. However, it was not long before Bernard became disgruntled with post-war England and, having had exposure to the Mediterranean climate, thought seriously about a move to warmer pastures. He and his wife eventually moved to Zimbabwe (then Rhodesia) in 1948, and for the next 16 years they lived in its capital, Salisbury, where they brought up their three sons. In 1964, after several unsettling experiences, Bernard and Rose made the decision to leave Rhodesia, seeking another continent altogether. Their first choice was Australia, and the family initially moved there. They remained there for four years, until the pull of Africa once again grew too strong. After a brief sojourn in Israel, they eventually settled permanently in Cape Town, South Africa.

In March of 1984, Martin Hirsch was married in London to Cynthia Posen, the niece of Henry Posen. Eight years previously, Martin's first wife had passed away, leaving Martin the formidable task of bringing up their eight children. Now he had found a helpmate.

In 1985, Mark Kay, the youngest son of Bernard and Rose Kay, moved to the big city of Johannesburg from Cape Town. Two years after that he was introduced to a young lady from Johannesburg, Linda Hirsch, daughter of Martin Hirsch and stepdaughter of Cynthia Posen. They were married shortly thereafter.

A few months after the wedding, Linda's stepmother Cynthia showed Mark a translation of a diary which had been written by her late uncle, Henry Posen. She knew that Mark was fascinated with that period and with the life stories of the people who lived then. As Mark went through the spellbinding transcript of Henry's history and experiences, he came to that section of the diary where Henry described his miraculous survival among the wreckage of the Andora Star and of his arrival in Scotland as a prisoner of war. It was at that point that Mark experienced an unusual sensation, as he read about the incident of Henry approaching the guard who was encircling the perimeter fence, and who Henry had recognized to be a Jew.

Mark had heard many times from his father about his experiences during the Second World War and he knew that his father had served in the Royal Scots Regiment. More significantly, he remembered his father describing a cold winter night somewhere in the north of Scotland, and an unusual meeting that he had had with a fellow Jew. With a rising feeling of excitement, Mark reached for the phone and began dialing his father. He had an amazing story to tell him.

Nearly half a century after a brave soldier helped out a fellow Jew, his son discovers that he is married to a relative of the very man his father helped.

(This story was reconstructed from Henry's diary with the help of Mark Kay.)

▪ Debt of Gratitude

Among the various categories of nonkosher foods is included the meat of an animal known as a treifah *(lit., torn)*. A treifah *is a kosher animal which was fatally wounded prior to slaughtering. The meat from such an animal is forbidden for a Jew to eat, even if the animal was subsequently slaughtered according to the* halachah. *The verse in the Torah tells us that rather than eating it, "you should throw it to the dog."*

Rashi, *using a technique in Talmudic logic known as a* kal v'chomer *(an a priori* argument), *proves that it is completely permissible to present* treifah *meat to a gentile, since he is permitted to consume such flesh. Thus there is no practical halachic distinction between presenting the* treifah *meat as a gift to one's non-Jewish business associate, for example, and feeding it to one's dog. The reason why the dog is singled out for this privilege is one which dates far back to the beginning*

*of our nation's history. Despite the chaos and uproar surround-
ing the tenth plague in Egypt, a clamor which under normal circumstances would certainly have whipped the resident canines
into a frenzy of barking and howling, on the night of the Plague
of the Firstborns there was silence in the Jewish neighborhoods.
At Hashem's behest, on the night of the tenth plague, the dogs
"bit their tongues." The result of their obedience was a great
Kiddush Hashem, a sanctification of Hashem's Name.*

*To these dogs, their descendants, and their relatives, we
are advised to cast our* treifah *meat. Although it may seem
to have been a small action on the part of the hounds in
Egypt, the Torah teaches us that Hashem does not withhold
the just reward of any creature.*

*If Hashem does not withhold reward from an obedient
hound, it is obvious that He will certainly compensate and
honor the good deeds of a human being, no matter how
small those deeds may seem to have been. The following
incident occurred to my brother and a close friend one
motz'aei Shabbos a short while ago.*

It was shortly after midnight, and Dani and Kevin were heading
home after a late meal at a popular kosher steak house. Dani
was at the wheel of the car, and as they neared the intersection of
Eleventh Avenue and the major arterial Louis Botha, he suddenly
slammed firmly on the brake pedal. Ahead of them, a vehicle was
standing at a bizarre angle on the edge of the road. It was only
when they spotted a second vehicle on the opposite side of the intersection, with two wheels on the curb and shards of glass
scattered around it, that they realized that there had been some
sort of collision. As they slowed their car to a halt, a young man
stumbled out from behind the nearer car, waving his arms hysterically to attract their attention.

Dani reached for his cellular phone. The young man was screaming for help, and seemed to be pointing to the far side of the car.
Next to the battered vehicle lay what appeared to be the driver, mo-

tionless and stained with blood. Dani knew exactly what was required, and without a second's hesitation, he clutched his cellular phone and began dialing the Johannesburg Hatzalah hot line.

Some three miles away, in a cozy Glenhazel home, the silence enveloping the slumbering form under a down quilt was shattered by the harsh trill of a cellular phone. The quilt heaved explosively as the surge of adrenalin rushed headlong through the veins of the volunteer dispatcher, and before the phone could utter its second shriek, he firmly pressed the answer button. "Hatzalah Medical Rescue, do you have an emergency?"

While the dispatcher jotted down the details from Dani, Kevin attempted to calm the two young casualties, who were by now shivering from a combination of shock and cold. Across the intersection, the second car stood silently, its occupants making no effort to exit the precariously parked vehicle. Dani finished the call and was suddenly struck by the overpowering stench of alcohol on the victim's breath. *There was no doubt as to the cause of this accident*, he thought as they waited for help to arrive.

The dispatcher's fingers trembled slightly as he furiously punched a series of digits into his phone. Then, he held the phone to his mouth and stated in his steadiest voice: "Attention all responders, we have a report of an MVA (Motor Vehicle Accident) at the intersection of Louis Botha and Eleventh. Two confirmed casualties, could be more. The time is 12:23. Please respond." He keyed in another few digits.

In scattered locations throughout the northern suburbs of Johannesburg, twenty-five cellular phones simultaneously burst into life with a ring, a buzz, or a garish melody. Twenty-five steady hands reached out from under blankets, from behind steering wheels, or into pockets to retrieve their noisy handsets. Thanks to the wonders of modern technology, the message recorded by the dispatcher only seconds before was heard simultaneously by all twenty-five of the Hatzalah volunteers.

Within a minute, two responders were on the scene. They had been in their cars when the call came through, and were not far from the scene at the time. While they carefully assessed the casualties, another eight volunteers were quickly buttoning up shirts and zipping up jackets, as they jumped into their cars and raced through the dark Johannesburg streets.

The men on the scene performed a hasty triage: The driver of the vehicle that Dani and Kevin had first come across was assigned Priority One (P1) status, entitling him to be treated first and by the most experienced personnel. His companion was suffering from shock and bruising, and was designated a P3, while the two occupants of the other vehicle were assessed to be P2s.

Ten minutes after placing the call, Dani stepped back to watch the inspiring scene unfolding in front of his eyes. Ten qualified paramedics, many of them highly experienced in the field, bustled purposefully around the injured figures lying alongside the two vehicles. Blood pressures, breathing rates, oxygen saturations, and sugar levels were quickly gauged; then, based on these results, intravenous lines were set up, dressings were applied, back braces assembled, and the patients stabilized. Watching the efficiency and confidence of the team, one might have thought they were working under the gleaming lights of a sterile operating room, rather than on the sidewalk of a city street by the light of a few streetlamps relieving the midnight darkness.

Another ten minutes passed before a distant wail was heard and the flashing red lights of the local ambulance appeared over the horizon, racing toward the intersection. Were it not for Hatzalah, the patients could quite easily have spent half an hour waiting on the sidewalk for help to arrive.

As Dani watched the ambulance slowly pull away from the scene, he wondered to himself what the young patients had done to deserve the unique and professional attention they had received. Two young gentiles, inebriated like flies in a wine vat, had nearly wiped themselves out in their intoxicated state. Then, ten of the most qualified Jewish doctors and paramedics had rushed to the scene and saved the lives of these two fools, at least one of whom would otherwise have bled to death on the side of the road. There was no doubt that Providence was on their side. The question that fascinated Dani was: Why? The answer was not long in coming.

The morning after the accident, Moshe Schneider received a phone call. Moshe, an experienced *shochet*, had been involved in the provision of kosher meat in Johannesburg for many years. When he answered the phone that morning, the voice on the other end was a familiar one, laced with a heavy Afrikaans accent. Moshe immediately recognized his caller, for he and the man had worked together for many years. The man's name was Gert Oberholzer, and he worked for a large meat-distributing company in Johannesburg. For some twenty years, Gert had been involved with the kosher-meat division of the company, and for twenty years it was Gert who had ensured that the Jewish community was adequately supplied with kosher meat.

"Moshe," said the man on the phone that morning, "I want to tell you what your people did for my boy last night." His normally stoic voice broke slightly as he told Moshe what had transpired. "If not for you Jews, my boy would have died last night. I just wanted to say thank you."

Moshe thought for a moment and replied, "Actually, Gert, it was our way of saying thank *you*!"

▪ Funeral Arrangement

There is much discussion among the various commentaries as to why our matriarch Sarah was in Hevron at the time of her passing, considering that she and Avraham were then residing in the town of Be'er Sheva.

My teacher, Rav Aharon Pfeuffer, zt"l, offered the following interpretation, based on the simple reading of the verses. Avraham journeyed together with Yitzchak from their town of Be'er Sheva to Har HaMoriah, found in present-day Jerusalem, a trip which took some three days. Along the way, they would have passed through, or nearby to, the city of Hevron, which lies between Be'er Sheva and Har HaMoriah. While the two of them were involved in the momentous test of the Akeidah at Har HaMoriah, Sarah became concerned as to what had become of her husband and son, and so she traveled northwards in the direction of Har HaMoriah, stopping in the town of Hevron en route. It was there that she received word of the Akeidah and it was there that she expired. Subsequently, Avraham and Yitzchak retraced their steps southwards, stopping in Hevron to grieve and to bury Sarah.

Most of the commentators concur that Sarah passed away at the time allotted to her, unlike Avraham, who expired five years before his designated time. The Malbim adds a fascinating extension to this idea, for he explains that not only did Sarah die at her predestined time, but also at a predestined place, the town of Hevron. The Malbim sums up this twist of Providence with a famous Tannaic idiom:

"A man's feet are his guarantors, for to the place where he is summoned [to die], there he is led" (Succah 53a).

The following incident occurred many years ago and was recounted to me by Rabbi Menachem Raff.

The small crowd was gathered at the West Park cemetery in Johannesburg to escort an elderly woman on her last earthly journey. She had lived well into her 90's, and three generations of her offspring were present that day to see her off, including three of her great-grandsons, all of whom had grown into fine young adults, proud of their Jewish heritage. Rabbi Menachem Raff, spiritual leader of the congregation with which her family was affiliated, was charged with conducting the ceremony, and the required quorum of ten was completed by a group of students from the religious school attended by the great-grandsons of the deceased. The ceremony was carried out in a dignified and reverent manner, the young Torah students adding to the honor and respect being paid to the departed. When the burial was over, the family, together with the rabbi and the group of students who had accompanied them, slowly wended their way through the graveyard, and once again entered the empty funeral hall.

As they headed for the door and the parking lot beyond, Rabbi Raff was called aside by one of the officials of the *Chevrah Kaddisha*, the Jewish Burial Society. A second funeral was about to begin, but there was not a *minyan* of mourners to accompany the woman to her grave, as is required by the *halachah*. When Rabbi Raff inquired as to how many people were present, the official pointed to a single young woman standing to one side. According to the official, the woman was a social worker who had occasionally visited the deceased in the hotel in which she had resided. Aside from her, no one had turned out for the funeral.

Rabbi Raff realized that a great *mitzvah* opportunity was presenting itself to him and his companions, and without hesitation he turned to the group of young students and asked them if they would stay. He added that it was a huge merit, one that seldom presents itself. The boys consented, and a moment later, they were joined by Rabbi Chaim Davidson, the rabbi commissioned by the *Chevrah Kaddisha* to perform the funeral. The service got under way, and for the second time in one day, the young group of neatly dressed Torah students gently lifted the coffin and headed out into the graveyard.

As they walked, Rabbi Raff turned to the officiating rabbi and asked him about the woman being buried. Perhaps the rabbi knew where she came from or what had become of her family and friends. Rabbi Raff was in fact trying to understand for himself how it came to be that a woman with no friends and family should end up being buried by a group of young Torah students, all of whom were already advanced in their studies and character development. The reply that he received from his colleague sent a chill up his spine.

The elderly woman had once been an exceptionally wealthy member of the community. According to Rabbi Davidson, she was much renowned for her generosity and benevolence, and had supported many Jewish institutions in the Johannesburg area. Tragically, her friends and family had all passed on before her, leaving her to die as a lonely woman.

As Rabbi Raff trod slowly behind the bier, he marveled to himself how it had come to be that this elderly woman received the last respect that she deserved. She had died alone, but was buried in a truly dignified way, by a handful of young men who were the fine products of the institutions she had once supported.

■ Living Proof

The Gemara in Shabbos (152b) relates an unusual story. Some laborers were digging in the property of the Sage Rav Nachman, when they came across the intact corpse of the Sage Rav Achai bar Yoshiah. The Gemara relates a dialogue which ensued between Rav Nachman and the corpse. (Maharal explains that this dialogue is in fact allegorical and refers to an inner dialogue which Rav Nachman had with himself as he contemplated the corpse.) At one point Rav Nachman said to the corpse, "Is it not written, 'And the dust shall return to the earth as it was'" (Koheles 12:7)? Clearly the Sage was puzzled by the fact that the body had not decomposed. Replied the corpse: He who taught you the book of Koheles apparently did not teach you the book of Mishlei for there (14:30) it states: "The rotting of bones is [caused by] envy," implying that whoever has envy in his heart during his lifetime, his bones will rot after his death, but whoever does not have envy in his heart while he is alive, his bones will not rot after his death."

The following story illustrates the benefits of not being envious of others and of being satisfied with one's lot. A person who is content will not be easily upset by others. I quote it as told to me by the person concerned.

My father, Yehudah Leib ben Binyamin Shap HaKohen, was born in Vilna on the 4th of Iyar in the year 1902. Not long after his arrival in the world, the situation in Europe began to deteriorate, and when he was 11 years old he and his father uprooted themselves from the place they called home and set sail for warmer and friendlier climes. Like many others who were fortunate enough to escape Europe before the upheavals began, Yehudah Leib and his father eventually found themselves washed up on the sunny shores of South Africa. Here they settled in the Eastern Cape province where my grandfather became a trader on a small, remote trading station called Ngwenya. At a very young age my father joined him in the business and quickly learned the rudiments of how to be a successful trader. When he married my mother a few years later, he bought a trading store in the nearby village, Debe Nek, where he worked for many years. In 1957, he sold the store and moved to Cape Town where they lived out the rest of their lives. He passed away on the 19th of Iyar in the year 1973, and was buried in Cape Town.

My father was a very gentle person who generally did not get angry. When the local black people would come to his shop to sell their wool or birdseed, he would be very particular about the weights with which he measured their produce. He would pay the right price but ensured that the scale was correct. Similarly, when selling them goods, he was just as particular, and would rather give the customer the benefit of a little more goods. Shortly after his passing, I received a beautiful letter from Dreyfus Fichla, a black teacher who lived in the town of Debe Nek during my father's time there. In painstaking English, he testified to my father's honesty and the respect that he had for all the people of Debe Nek:

> Dear Madam,
> I am quite sure you may not recognize or remember who I am. I will introduce myself as one of your father's best customers at Debe Nek. I was known to the late Mr. Louis Shap as early as 1920 and until he left Debe Nek. He was my inti-

mate dealer. When he left he went [sic] to my home to shake hands and he would not be happy if he did not come to say good-bye before leaving Debe Nek...He was a very honest man and he honored friendship not with whites only but with black people in particular. He studied the needs of his customers and extended great sympathy to each and every customer. He was really an honest dealer, and very courteous indeed. He used to say, "Friendship is more than money." He used to say that he would rather lose money than lose friendships. He believed that if he can have no friends he was a poor man but if [he] has many friends he was a rich man!

When selling articles to a customer he would never sell what he knew was not quite genuine even if the customer thought it was good ... He never sued his customers – oh not once!

During the world war we used to gather in his lounge listening to the radio news about the war. That was the only European home where we could do such a thing...

How can we not mourn for such a friend and helper. I have never seen him angry and saying bad words to anyone.

Yours faithfully,
Dreyfus Fichla
Debe Nek

My mother passed away nearly twenty years after my father. In a codicil to her last will and testament, she wrote that she wished to be buried in Israel. In deference to her wishes, my husband and I, together with my brothers, made plans to accompany her to Israel on her last earthly journey. On the *Motz'aei Shabbos* prior to our leaving Johannesburg, my rabbi and teacher, Rav Aharon Pfeuffer, *z"tl*, visited me to offer his condolences. In the course of our discussion, he asked me where my father was buried. When I told him that he had been buried in Cape Town nineteen years previously, the rabbi told me, "You are not obligated to do so, but it would be correct for you to move your father to Eretz Yisrael."

My mother was laid to rest in the Holy Land on the 26th of Cheshvan. While sitting *shivah* at my daughter's house in Jerusalem, I told my two brothers of the advice of Rabbi Pfeuffer. Both instantly agreed to the plan.

On my arrival back in South Africa, we set about making the necessary arrangements. Unfortunately however, the *Chevrah Kaddisha* in Cape Town could not give us an exact date for the disinterment but said it would be before the following Pesach.

The week before Pesach they phoned to say that it was not possible to have it done before Pesach as they had six funerals that week, and promised to exhume my father's remains at some point after the festival. In the course of the phone call they also asked if we would mind "to have the remains placed in a child's coffin." I was aghast at the thought, and although we consented, I prayed silently, "Hashem, please don't let it be like that."

After Pesach we were told that my father had been exhumed and that his remains would be flown to Israel. My daughter and son-in-law flew to Israel to be present at the reburial. They described how initially a respectful silence filled the air at the graveside. Suddenly a noise rose from the members of the *Chevrah Kaddisha*, and a voice exclaimed: "*Er iz a tzaddik, er is beshleimus, hit zach der fies* — This man is a tzaddik, his body is complete, watch your feet." My daughter asked her husband to go and see what was going on. On his return to Johannesburg, I asked him what he had seen. He told me: "Mom, I have a weak stomach, but I thought they were finished, and when I looked they were changing his *tachrichim* [burial shrouds]. He looked like the picture on your wall."

I phoned Rav Pfeuffer immediately to tell him of the remarkable occurrence, that my father's remains had not disintegrated after nearly twenty years. He told me of the aforementioned Gemara in *Maseches Shabbos* which states that someone who is not envious and stingy will not be eaten by worms.

My father was reburied at Har Menuchos in Jerusalem on the 12th of Iyar.

I later spoke to Rabbi Yissachar Frand, telling him about this miracle with my father. I also told him that my father was a very honest man. Rabbi Frand turned to me and said, "I am not a *chassid* but I would like to show you something." He took a *Chumash* and read aloud the *pasuk* from *Parashas Ki Seitzei* : "*Even shleimah vatzedek* — A perfect and honest weight shall you have, a perfect and honest measure shall you have, so that your days shall be lengthened on the land that Hashem, your God, gives you" (*Devarim* 25:15).

Our family was in Israel for my niece's wedding during that year, and we unveiled the two tombstones of my parents. Incredibly, the *parashah* of that week was *Ki Seitzei*.

▪ Kaddish

When the Torah describes the call for donations from the Israelites toward the Mishkan *(Tabernacle), it uses the word* v'nasnu *which means "and they shall give." The word* v'nasnu *is spelled* vav, nun, saf, nun, vav. *What is exceptional about this word is that it is a palindrome, meaning that it can be read in either direction without changing its meaning. This comes to teach you that what a person gives to charity will return to him, and he will not lose anything because of this giving. Giving, although it may seem to be a one-way street, is in fact highly profitable. What you give away, you get back, and for the original giving you get a* mitzvah *for helping out a fellow Jew (Ba'al HaTurim).*

The Talmud tells us that one should tithe his money in order to become wealthy. It goes on to explain that although we are generally not permitted to "test" G-d, in this particular area it is permitted. The pasuk *brought to prove this reads: "Test Me, if you will, with this, says Hashem, Master of Legions, [see] if I do not open up for you the windows of the heavens and pour out upon you blessing without end" (Ta'anis 9a).*

Giving does not always involve reaching for one's wallet. There are times when a helping hand, a shoulder to cry on, or an encouraging smile are far greater gifts than money. To act is to give too, and these actions surely do not go unrewarded. This was the experience of one of the residents of my neighborhood, as described to me by a close mutual friend.

M ike Rabin's entry into the world of religious Judaism was a gradual one by most standards. At age 55 his life was well established despite the absence of any personal belief or, in his opinion, thanks to that absence. *Religion was for people who don't have worthwhile things to do on a Saturday morning,* he reassured himself repeatedly. It took a couple of years before he began taking his first hesitant steps along the path so well worn by the *ba'alei teshuvah* of our generation. Within a short while he had his kitchen *kashered* and began observing the Jewish dietary laws, together with his wife and three daughters. Next, he began saying *Tehillim* and not long after that, Mike purchased a beautiful pair of *tefillin* for himself and began attending shul three times a day. Suddenly religion had become the focus of his life around which everything else revolved. Finally, he moved his family into a new residence, all so that they would be able to walk to the synagogue on Shabbos. When Mike commits himself to a project, he doesn't believe in half measures.

Mike is a punctilious man, and he committed himself to praying with a *minyan* whenever possible: *Shacharis* every morning, proudly adorned in his new *tefillin*; *Minchah* and *Ma'ariv* every evening, with a Torah-study session in between. He became more familiar with the regular attendees of the shul than with his business colleagues, and he loved every moment of his newfound lifestyle.

One evening, he noticed a young man sitting in the shul, looking forlorn and dejected. Mike sensed that the man needed some warmth and an ear to confide in, so he approached the slouching figure and seated himself in the next pew. When the man finally looked up, Mike could see that he was not much older than 20. His eyes were red as though he had been crying. "What troubles you, my son?" Mike asked quietly as he gently placed his hand on the young man's shoulder. The man didn't flinch, but in his eyes Mike could see the turmoil silently raging.

The two men sat quietly for a few moments until the young man finally succumbed to the therapeutic relief of sharing the load weighing down his heart. He cleared his throat and whispered, "I lost my dad last week." He bit his bottom lip and his chin trembled as he tried to hold back the tears. More silence. "I haven't said *Kaddish* yet."

He fought his emotions for a few more seconds and then blurted, "I actually don't know how."

Mike squeezed the young man's shoulder lightly, and waited for him to bring his emotions under control. Then he said, "I want you to know that many years ago, I also lost my dad. I also didn't know how to say *Kaddish*. I had a friend who sat with me and taught me how to do it, every word and sound. We practiced it until I knew it perfectly. And then I was able to say *Kaddish* for my father."

The man was staring into Mike's eyes.

"It would be such a tremendous privilege if you would allow me to teach you *Kaddish*, as my friend once did for me."

The young man blinked and nodded slowly.

"You're gonna need a *siddur*," Mike said, pointing to the book-shelf on the other side of the shul. "Let's go find you one."

The two walked up to the bookshelf. On the way the young man told Mike that his name was David Eliasov and that he almost never came to shul. It was the first time since his father's passing that he had taken the plunge. "Which one should I take?" he asked as they stood in front of the full shelf of books. "Whichever one you want," replied Mike. "They are all the same." The boy stuck out his hand and pulled a *siddur* from the shelf. He opened the front cover and suddenly began to sob uncontrollably. Mike was mystified by the sudden mood change, and once again he draped his arm over David's shoulder. When the sobbing finally stopped, Mike asked what it was that had disturbed him so much. David didn't reply, but instead he opened the *siddur* and pointed to the inside of the front cover. There was inscribed: "This *siddur* was donated to the shul by Robert Eliasov." A chill ran up Mike's spine. David sat very still and his eyes took on a faraway look. "I remember my dad once telling me that he had donated a book to the shul. He was not a religious man but he was very proud of his contribution."

Mike was flabbergasted. A single book out of an entire bookshelf, and a grieving son had picked the right one!

They returned to the shul and together they went through the Mourner's Prayer. At *Ma'ariv*, David Eliasov recited *Kaddish* flawlessly — from the siddur "belonging" to his father.

A week later, Mike's daughter Shelley was driving home along Louis Botha Avenue on her way from visiting her parents. She was thinking dreamily about her upcoming marriage. A traffic light up ahead suddenly flicked from green to yellow, waking her from her reverie. Instinctively her right foot plunged onto the brake pedal. She managed to bring the car to a halt in time, but unfortunately the driver behind her was not as quick with his reflexes. The big car plowed into the back of her small Honda. All Shelley heard was the screech of tires followed by a massive bang and the sound of shattering glass.

Fortunately the damage was limited to the body and windows of the two cars, although Shelley's nerves were considerably shattered as well. A young man who happened to be passing by helped the shaken young woman out of the damaged vehicle. He then directed her out of the way of the traffic, and quickly dialed for help on his mobile phone. After helping her deal with the police report and assisting with arrangements for a towing service to pick up the damaged car, he then approached her again and asked if there was anyone whom she wanted him to call. She was overwhelmed by the man's thoughtfulness, and thanked him profusely before asking him to dial her parents. When Mike heard what had happened, it took the young man a few minutes to reassure him that his daughter was unhurt. Mike thanked the man effusively for his help, and promised to be there as soon as possible. Five minutes later Mike pulled up at the scene of the accident, and as he stepped out of his car, his jaw fell.

"David Eliasov!" he called out to his daughter's savior, "It's so good to see you again!"

David Eliasov was exceptionally moved by the serendipitous opportunity which allowed him to repay the kindness Mike had bestowed on him. As a result of that inspiration, added to his "chance" discovery of the book his father had donated to the shul, David committed himself to accompany Mike to shul every day to recite *Kaddish* for his late father.

▪ Masai-mara Miracle

The Sfas Emes, the famous Rebbe of Gur, recounts an insight of his grandfather, known as the Chiddushei HaRim, into a famous statement of the Talmud in Megillah. It is taught that one who claims, "I have toiled and I did not find," or one who claims, "I did not toil yet I found," should not be believed. However, if he claims to have toiled and found, he is to be trusted. This is a wise and accurate observation, yet one could ask why it is that this person who did indeed toil used the word "found" to describe his success, implying that it was almost by chance that he came across his success and not as a result of his effort. Surely it would be more accurate to claim to have toiled and "achieved."

The Chiddushei HaRim answered that the successes of a person are not directly proportional to his efforts. If he toils with unswerving dedication, he will "chance upon" much more than just simple achievement, for Hashem assists those who aspire. Indeed, if a person toils, he will find.

My cousin Michael Esra dearly wanted to do a mitzvah, but it seemed as if circumstances were going to prevent him. This is the story he told me.

For as long as he could remember, Michael had dreamed of visiting Kenya. The lure of this East African country was not a rational one, and had nothing to do with the cities or people to be found there. Something deep inside of him yearned to experience the great wilderness, the vastness of the famous Serengeti which straddles Kenya's southern border with Tanzania, to be able to look to the horizon and beyond and see nothing but waving plains of African grassland. There is something profoundly humbling about experiencing such grandeur and expanse, and it is a universal human trait to seek such experiences. Perhaps it gives us an opportunity to realign ourselves with the universe, to put ourselves into some sort of cosmic proportion.

Consequently, when an opportunity for such a trip came up a few months after his marriage to his wife Rayna, Michael needed little convincing. He met with the travel agent in June, and booked six places on an organized tour of the parks of Kenya for December of the same year. Next he called two of his friends who had also recently married and invited them to accompany Rayna and him. The couples were delighted by the invitation and readily agreed.

As the year slowly wended its way toward December, Michael felt the excitement rising inside of him. It was about a month before they were scheduled to leave that his bubble burst and a most terrible realization dawned on him. Michael had lost his father a few years before, and his *yahrtzeit* always fell out in late December or early January. A perfunctory examination of the calendar proved his worst fears true; the calendar confirmed that he would be somewhere in Kenya at the time of the *yahrtzeit*. He consulted the itinerary provided by his travel agent and was even more disturbed to find that they would be somewhere in the heart of the Masai-Mara game reserve on the date his father had died.

For the next few days, Michael grappled with one of the hardest dilemmas he had ever faced. On the one hand he felt a strong sense of responsibility toward the *mitzvah* of reciting *Kaddish* in the presence of a *minyan* on the *yahrtzeit*, one of the few formal opportunities a child gets to honor his father posthumously. On the other hand, he realized that if he were to pull out of the tour, the entire expedition would fold and he would be letting the other two couples down, not to mention the fact that he was desperate to make the trip himself. In the end it was the latter arguments which triumphed, and Michael chose not to even mention the matter to his traveling partners. With a niggling feeling of guilt, Michael set about preparing and packing for the trip.

The Masai-Mara, or "Mara" as it is affectionately known, is Kenya's small share of the evocative and expansive Serengeti, one of the largest grassland regions in Africa which occupies a large chunk of northern Tanzania. The Mara is populated by an abundance of game, which dot the rolling grasslands otherwise only punctuated by the occasional acacia or "umbrella" tree. Because of its vast size, some 320 square kilometers, most tour operators prefer to show it to their guests "safari style," hopping from one lodge to another and covering great distances each day. In this way the tourists get to see a large part of the reserve. Michael and his party spent three nights in the park, each night sleeping in a different hotel.

Yahrtzeit for Michael's father fell on the third night of their stay in the park. The hotel was very empty, for the peak tourist season was over. The six friends were sitting in the lobby of the hotel enjoying an early evening drink, when one of them noticed that Michael was unusually quiet and reserved. At first he was unwilling to divulge the reason for his gloominess, but after some gentle prodding from the others he eventually let it all out. He told them of his difficult decision, and how this would be the first year that he would miss saying *Kaddish* because the nearest *minyan* was hundreds of miles away. His friends tried to ease his mind but Michael was unable to shake the feelings of guilt.

They were still discussing Michael's predicament when the large doors of the hotel swung open and a noisy crowd piled into the lobby. They approached the front desk and began checking in boisterously. For a minute the South Africans studied them intently, and then without any explanation, Michael jumped out of his seat and approached the leader of the tour. He negotiated with the man for a moment and then returned to his friends with a flabbergasted but triumphant look spread across his face. The tourists were all Israelis. Michael hadn't found a *minyan*. The *minyan* had found him.

Minutes later, seven Israeli men balancing handkerchiefs awkwardly on their heads clustered together in the lobby of the hotel to complete a *minyan* for the "crazy South African" and his two friends. As Michael recited *Kaddish* deep in the Masai-Mara game reserve, a strange, warm feeling of contentment came over him.

He got his *minyan*, and to this day has never missed a *Kaddish*.

▪ Ana Avda

When we hear of the concept of mesirus nefesh *or self-sacrifice for the sake of our beliefs, the images which spring to mind generally revolve around anti-Semitism and oppression. These will include images of the Holocaust, Spanish inquisition, and the numerous pogroms which have stained our history with the blood of our brethren for thousands of years. There is no doubt that these are prime examples of self-sacrifice, highlighting the readiness of many Jewish individuals to trade everything, including their lives, for their beliefs. There is however another form of* mesirus nefesh, *a far more common type and one which may not seem as heroic as the aforementioned ones. Each and every day, thousands of Jews make tremendous sacrifices in order to observe the will of Hashem, a type of* mesirus nefesh *which is alive and well even in our times.*

The following is an unusual example, and one which demonstrates the direct and daily involvement of Hashem in the lives of those who cleave to Him.

It was close to 3 o'clock in the morning, and the normally bustling city of Bnei Brak slumbered quietly after yet another vibrant and chaotic day. The calm would not last for long though, for in only two short hours, the more energetic of her citizens would begin scurrying through her streets, headed for sunrise prayer gatherings, learning sessions, and places of work. In Bnei Brak there is little time for sleep.

In an apartment block not far from the famous Ponevezh Yeshivah, one man could not succumb to the soporific influence of the sleeping city. For Rav Aharon Pfeuffer the city was far from unfamiliar, yet on that warm night something would not let him sleep. It had been a few years since he had last visited the city of his youth, for his position of Rabbi and *posek* of a small community in Johannesburg kept him occupied for much of the year. Now, many years after leaving Israel to teach and lead in the Diaspora, he once again found himself savoring the sights and sounds of the Holy Land.

After tossing and turning for close to an hour, he conceded defeat, hopped out of his bed, and impulsively began to dress. A walk would probably clear his head, he decided to himself. He quietly closed the door of the flat, and descended to the street.

The city seemed eerily empty as he meandered along the sidewalk. The absence of pedestrians or vehicles made the place feel unnatural, as if the life had been drained out of the city, leaving behind an inert shell. He walked slowly down the street, following some unconscious tug that was gently pulling him toward his alma mater, the Ponevezh Yeshivah. Curiosity welled up inside of him, for it is seldom that one gets to see the giant study hall of the venerable institution not seething with energetic young students. On any given day, the voices of hundreds of young men unite to form a roar which can be heard from a distance, from early in the morning until late at night, as they toil over large tomes in their quest for the truth. The building was quiet as he slowly mounted the stairs leading up to the *beis midrash*.

As he entered the hall a wondrous sight confronted his eyes. At the front of the cavernous room, the famous golden *aron kodesh* glowed spectacularly, as if charged by the holy scrolls it protected. At the feet of the ark, hundreds of benches and lecterns stood in orderly rows, awaiting the young warriors who would in but a few hours do battle there. Rav Pfeuffer stood mesmerized by the scene.

Suddenly, he heard a sound. A strange haunting melody emanated from the front of the hall. Cautiously he walked forward, curiosity overriding any fear he might have felt. He stopped again to listen. There was no doubt that it was a human voice, and as he listened, he realized that the voice was singing. Presently, he spotted a young man sitting on one of the benches, swaying gently as he sang to himself. Rav Pfeuffer strained his ears to catch the words, treading softly so as not to disturb the singer, until he was close enough to identify the tune. The moving notes sent a shiver up his spine:

"Ana, Ana, Ana — Avda deKudesha Berich Hu,
Ana, Ana, Ana — Avda deKudesha Berich Hu."

"I, I, I — am a servant of the Holy One, Blessed is He."

Rav Pfeuffer was rooted to the spot, as over and over the man sang the famous declaration of faith, his eyes closed in concentration and devotion. Rav Pfeuffer stood there for what seemed like an eternity, taking in the power of the moment in the empty *beis midrash,* wondering what it was that had brought the man there at such an unearthly hour.

After a while, he sat down next to the man. The young man barely flinched as he opened his eyes to see a complete stranger sitting by his side. After a minute of silence Rav Pfeuffer inquired, *"Chaveri, hakol beseder?* — "My friend, is everything okay?"

The man hesitated momentarily and then, sensing that he could trust the rabbi, he told him his story:

"Only a few hours ago, I celebrated my wedding," the man said dramatically. "After the wedding, we had a question with regard to laws of family purity. It was already far too late for us to ask anyone, so we decided that I should come here and wait until I could ask someone to decide the question."

Among his numerous accomplishments, Rav Pfeuffer happened to be one of the great authorities of his era on the subject of these delicate and complex laws. After hearing and contemplating all the details of the particular case, Rav Pfeuffer decided that the question was unfounded and sent the young man back home.

Suddenly, it became obvious to the rabbi why sleep had eluded him that night. The Hand of Providence had ensured that a sleepless rabbi was in the right place at the right time to help a valiant young man in his time of need.

On his arrival back in South Africa, Rav Pfeuffer, zt"l, related the story to many of his students, citing it as a most inspiring example of the simple faith and commitment of the Jewish people to Hashem's will. He also taught them the song, together with the haunting tune he had heard in the empty *beis midrash* on that fateful night in Bnei Brak. It was from one of these students that I heard this most inspiring story.

▪ A Brief Note on Israel

To attempt to précis the character and essence of the geographical locality known to many simply as "The Holy Land" would be to do this tiny country the most terrible injustice. It borders on impossible to attempt such a description, and instead I will try to sum it up by illustrating two ubiquitous phenomena which can be found within her borders.

The standard Jerusalem Egged bus is a perfect microcosmic sample of the country in which it can be found. Packed into its confines, a hundred cultures collide with one another, merging to form the most bizarre yet vibrant mulch of seething humanity. Only in the standard Jerusalem roadside schwarma does one find a similar mix, a combination of Mediterranean, African, European, and American, among others, all precariously held together within the soggy sides of a piece of leaven. And at the helm of the Egged bus, a figure attempts to steer the throng toward its destiny, convinced that it is he giving the vehicle its direction, unaware of the fact that each member of the crowd behind him is of the same conviction. All of them, in turn, remain oblivious to the fact that it is only by the grace of G-d that they still find themselves heading toward some viable destination. Every Israeli bus driver is adamant that he would make the perfect prime minister.

It is only aboard one of these buses that one truly understands what Israel is all about. In the words of one of the many people I interviewed, "Everywhere in the world you can tune in and hear Hashem speaking to you, but it is only in Israel that one is truly next to the transmitter."

Indeed it would seem that the signal in Israel is much clearer.

▪ Hijacked

Belief in the existence of hashgachah pratis, or individual Divine attention, is one of the fundamentals of Judaism. Should we fail to understand and integrate this concept into our lives, the consequences can be disastrous. There is a section in the Torah that describes terrible curses which can befall the Jewish people. According to many of the commentators, these curses come if we relate to the goings-on in the world as "haphazard," refusing to see Hashem's direct, day-to-day involvement in our lives.

We must remember that every event is planned and coordinated down to the smallest detail, on a day-by-day, minute-by-minute, and even second-by-second basis. The following story illustrates this concept perfectly, and was related to me personally by the person concerned.

Night after night the dreams returned to haunt her. Bizarre images tormented her slumbering mind, leaving her tense and exhausted by the time the sun finally crept over the horizon to release her from her nightmares. Her husband, not wishing to cause more consternation than necessary, downplayed her concerns and tried his utmost to allay her growing fear. The dreams persisted. She learned to ignore them — until that fateful Saturday night when the situation reached its breaking point. This time the dream woke her. The details were too vivid, a terrifying incident involving close family members. Trembling with fear and trepidation, she turned to her husband and implored him to help her find a solution. "I can't go on like this!" she sobbed.

Danny and Helen Malkin were born in Johannesburg. Both spent their entire youth in the warm African climes, and it was only after the young couple married that they decided to head for the Holy Land and make *aliyah*. As a highly qualified and talented eye surgeon, Danny quickly gained respect in the city of Bnei Brak where they chose to settle, and within a short time, the soft-spoken doctor had created a name for himself among his patients and all those who came into contact with him. In the course of his work, Dr. Malkin also had the opportunity to treat some of the generation's most distinguished and respected rabbis. Close relationships developed, many of which he still maintains today.

Left with no other choice, Danny decided to take his wife's problem to one of the *gedolim*. Normally, his daily schedule did not allow for early-morning engagements, but on the morning after his wife's terrible nightmare, an opening happened to crop up "coincidentally." Immediately after *davening Shacharis*, Danny knocked on the door of Rav Yitzchak Zilberstein, *shlita*, Rav of the Ramat Elchanan neighborhood in Bnei Brak and one of the world's leading contemporary halachic experts. Rav Zilberstein was busy taking off his *tefillin* when a worried-looking Danny entered. The smile which resides almost permanently on the venerable Rabbi's countenance was immediately replaced by a look of concern. He greeted Danny warmly and asked what it was that was troubling him. He listened carefully as Danny related the details of Helen's recurring dreams, and of the final episode which had prompted Danny to visit him.

After hearing of Helen's reaction, Rav Zilberstein beckoned for Danny to come closer. He picked up the *tefillin* he had been wearing moments before and placed them in Danny's hands. "These are special *tefillin*," he said. "They belonged to the Steipler, truly one of the giants of the last generation." As Danny clasped the treasured phylacteries, the venerable Rabbi instructed him to recite certain chapters of *Tehillim* on behalf of his wife, followed by the special prayer that we say on festivals to be spared from the effects of bad dreams. After doing as he was instructed, Danny returned the *tefillin* to the Rabbi, thanked him warmly for his time, and departed. That night the dreams stopped.

Both Danny and Helen had close family living in South Africa. Helen's brother Arthur, an accomplished building contractor, was involved at the time in the holy task of building a *mikveh* for the growing religious community in Johannesburg. Not content to simply build the *mikveh*, Arthur gave his whole being to ensure that the *mikveh* was constructed according to the highest possible standards.

Three days after the meeting with Rav Zilberstein, the Malkins received a call from South Africa. It was Arthur, with an amazing story to tell. One morning, on his arrival at the *mikveh* site, he was approached by a group of men. Thinking that they were just vagrants looking for work, Arthur paid little attention to them. Suddenly, guns appeared, and before he knew it, the "vagrants" were holding him at gunpoint. Stunned, his mind went blank as he tried to think of what to do. A cold sweat broke out across his forehead. "These men are capable of anything," he thought to himself. Brandishing their weapons menacingly, the thugs instructed him to load up his brand-new van with all the tools he had at the site. This having been completed, the thieves piled into his vehicle and roared off, leaving Arthur standing trembling on the pavement, minus one car but thankful to be alive.

The rest of the phone conversation went something like this:

Danny: "Thank Heaven you are around to tell the tale; you must be feeling terribly shaken."

Arthur: "Yeah, but as you say, the main thing is that I'm alive and well."

Danny: "When did you say all this happened?"

Arthur: "Sunday, Sunday morning about 8:20."

A cold chill raced down Danny's spine. On Sunday morning at 8:20 he had been standing in front of Rav Zilberstein — with the Steipler's *tefillin* in his hands.

▪ Russian Roulette

We regularly praise and extol Hashem for the remarkable care and concern that He shows for the poor and indigent. Every morning in our prayers we describe how "He does justice for the exploited, He gives bread to the hungry…Hashem protects the strangers; orphan and widow He encourages."

Importantly, the refinement of our own character traits is to be done, according to our Sages, by means of emulation of Hashem's traits. In the words of the Talmud (Shabbos 133b), "Be like Him, just as He is gracious and merciful, you too should be gracious and merciful."

The following story, described to me by a colleague, demonstrates the exquisite timing and synchronization used by the Coordinator of everything to look after those who might feel uncomfortable and alienated, and of the remarkable opportunity given to us to be partners in that process and to learn from His ways.

Aran Cohen was studying in a yeshivah in Israel, and one spring day he found himself squeezed into a small vinyl seat on a crowded Egged bus, wending its way through the bustling streets of Jerusalem. As the bus lumbered through the center of town, Aran reflected on the upcoming festival of Pesach, and more importantly, on the fact that he had not yet found himself a Haggadah.

The bus turned into Jaffa Street and roared up the hill toward the famous Machaneh Yehudah fresh-produce market, a chaotic gathering of stalls and tiny shops frequented by hundreds of Jerusalemites who come there to purchase all their needs— from herring to hairbrushes and everything in between. As the bus rounded the corner and came to a halt, his attention was drawn to the display window of an ancient-looking bookshop, in which some Haggadahs were being exhibited. Paying little heed to his ultimate destination, he alighted from the bus to investigate the merchandise.

After perusing the various versions offered in the store, Aran settled on a Haggadah compiled by Rabbi Mattisyahu Glazerson, an author whom he happened to know personally. He paid for the volume and happily made his way back to the bus stop to resume his journey on the next bus.

The bus pulled up at the stop, and Aran climbed the stairs and paid the driver. Before he found a seat, he noticed a familiar face on the bus. It was Rabbi Glazerson, the compiler of the Haggadah which he had purchased moments earlier. As the bus pulled away from the curb, he staggered down the aisle to greet the rabbi and to tell him of the remarkable serendipity of their meeting.

After hearing Aran's tale, Rabbi Glazerson mentioned that he was actually on his way back from the printers, where he had concluded the printing of a Russian translation of the Haggadah. After a moment's thought, he pressed a copy into Aran's hand, and told him to give it to one of the Russian students in his yeshivah for Pesach. Aran had started his journey without a single Haggadah, and by a remarkable twist of *hashgachah pratis*, had arrived at his destination with not one, but two, new Haggadahs.

Over the next few days, Aran approached the various Russian students in the yeshivah, and was disappointed to find that all of them had already procured haggadahs for themselves. As Pesach neared, it appeared as if his fortuitous acquisition would go to waste, and that the fairy-tale nature of its acquisition would not end "happily ever after." A few days before the festival, he set the Haggadah aside and promptly forgot about it as he resumed his preparations for the *chag*.

The festival arrived and after *davening Ma'ariv* on Seder night, Aran's teacher, Rabbi Chaim Raff, approached him. After wishing him the traditional "*Gut Yom Tov*," the rabbi turned to him with an unusual request. Did Aran know where he could get a Russian translation of the Haggadah? The rabbi's parents-in-law had invited a family of Russian immigrants for the Seder, and had overlooked the fact that they might need a Russian Haggadah to feel part of the service.

Aran was overjoyed to be able to present him with the Russian Haggadah, a book that was clearly not destined to spend a lonely Seder night on his own shelf.

▪ Taken for a Ride

"The sins that you commit against your fellow man are not atoned for on Yom Kippur unless you placate him, as it says, 'You will be cleansed of all your sins before G-d.' This means that only sins against G-d are atoned for on Yom Kippur, but sins committed against your neighbor are not atoned for unless you placate your neighbor [first] ... And even if you sinned against your friend only with words, you must appease him. It is your duty to personally appease him..." (Kitzur Shulchan Aruch 131).

"One who comes to purify himself, assistance is given to him" (Shabbos 104a).

The following story was told one Shabbos afternoon in the shul where I daven by a friend who had just returned from Eretz Yisrael. I later visited his home to get the finer details from him. This is the story he told.

When it comes to negotiating the bustling streets of inner-city Jerusalem, any seasoned tourist knows that to maneuver one's own car can be extremely detrimental to one's health. The mental strain and emotional angst generated by a short trip downtown would almost certainly warrant a bold-print warning from the Surgeon General, were it not for the fact that the described condition affects only foreigners, and is hence not within the Israeli health department's jurisdiction. As a result of these inherent cardiac and neurological hazards, the average tourist frequenting these parts has at his disposal two primary intercity travel options, these being the ubiquitous Egged bus or the more exclusive but often slower white taxicab.

Ian Smolowitz is a seasoned tourist. Over the years he has traveled countless times from his hometown of Johannesburg to Jerusalem, and he is all too familiar with the nature of the city's transport. For years he willingly patronized both the bus and taxi fraternities, happy to regularly pay the premium for a cab in exchange for the convenience and luxury of his own "chauffeur-driven" Mercedes, the likes of which prowl the streets of Jerusalem.

Then, on one of his trips to the Holy Land, Ian began to feel that perhaps he was being taken advantage of. He found that the cab drivers consistently refused to employ their taximeters, insisting instead that he pay a flat rate which always appeared to be inflated. By the end of that trip, Ian made up his mind to boycott the cabs on any future visits, and to stick to the less exclusive but more honest bus service.

The next year Ian once again found himself in Eretz Yisrael, this time to visit his recently married son and daughter-in-law, their newborn baby, and his other son who was learning in yeshivah at the time. On this particular occasion, he checked into a downtown hotel, conveniently situated halfway between each of his sons' institutions of higher learning, with the intention of spending the mornings studying with one son and the afternoons with the other.

On the first day, things did not start out so well. It began with an early morning call from South Africa bearing two pieces of bad news. The first concerned the demise of a close friend's father under difficult circumstances, while the second piece of information was regarding the sudden collapse of the South African currency, which had unexpectedly plummeted to R13,68 to the dollar. This was a major blow to Ian's income, for Ian's company back in South Africa was largely import based, and all his stock was paid for in dollars, but sold in rands. Furthermore, he realized that every dollar he would subsequently spend on his travels was worth a fortune in rands, a sobering thought.

After spending the morning learning with his married son in the Old City, Ian was scheduled to be on the opposite side of town at his younger son's yeshivah, and was running late. As Ian rushed through the cobbled streets of the Old City, he realized that he would be unacceptably late if he was to wait for a bus. With a sinking feeling he realized that he would have to take a cab, something he dearly did not want to do, even before the news of the rand's collapse.

A white Mercedes screeched to a halt almost before he had raised his finger in the traditional manner. Ian grudgingly tugged at the door handle, sank into the back seat, and closed the door behind him. As the driver pulled away from the curb, Ian leaned forward and in his most commanding Hebrew, barked:

"Put the meter on! To Bayit Vegan! No funny business!"

The driver made as if he wanted to reply, but before he found the words Ian was at him again:

"Don't try anything, my friend! I'm tired of being taken for a ride by you taxi drivers."

"*Shalom Aleichem*, my friend," said the cabdriver.

Ian barely gave him a chance. "You probably think I am an American and that I've got lots of money. Well, I'm not American and my money's worth nothing now!"

The day's frustration, combined with his fear of being ripped off, came tumbling out of Ian's mouth. Only when Ian had finished his tirade did the driver speak.

"My friend, do you not believe in saying '*Shalom Aleichem*, Moshe,' or perhaps even 'How are you, Moshe?'" Ian fell silent.

"Perhaps you might want to ask, 'How is your family, Moshe?' or maybe inquire how I am feeling after defending the Jewish people of Hevron during my army call-up last week," the driver demanded. Ian felt his ears reddening.

"You think that I am making lots of money doing this job, do you? You should know that I can barely feed my family with the money I make. Since the new Intifada began, the planes are landing empty at Ben Gurion. There are no more tourists. Do you know what my colleagues and I would give to live the way you do back in South Africa? And all you can do is shout at me as if I'm going to rip you off."

For the remainder of their journey across the Holy City, Ian begged the man to forgive him for his insensitivity, but was met with a stony refusal. Moshe the cabdriver would not forgive him, and continued to berate Ian until he stepped out of the cab in the suburb of Bayit Vegan. Ian was distraught.

The remainder of the day passed like a dark cloud. Ian sat with his son in the buzzing study hall of the yeshivah, the open Gemara in front of his nose, its crisp black letters slightly out of focus. Ian's mind was elsewhere. When he finally got back to his room that night, his wife inquired of his day, and the entire story came tumbling out. She sympathized with his predicament, but tried to encourage him to put the incident behind him. "The taxi driver has probably forgotten about the entire episode," she offered, but Ian was inconsolable. That night he struggled to sleep, tossing and turning as he recalled the stony face of Moshe the taxi driver, the man whom he had treated so insensitively, the man who had refused to forgive him.

The next morning, after *Shacharis* and breakfast in the hotel, Ian descended to the street level to arrange transport to the Old City. As he stood outside the hotel, he studied the faces in the passing taxicabs in the hope that he might recognize the face of the driver. He wanted to find Moshe. He had to obtain forgiveness from him. After a while Ian realized that it was a futile effort, and he was about to hail a cab, when someone tapped him on the shoulder. It was one of the guests from the hotel. He had succeeded in organizing a shuttle bus from the hotel to the Old City, and wanted to invite Ian aboard. Ian thanked the man and gratefully followed him toward the bus.

Ian was immersed in his own sorry thoughts as he mounted the steps of the bus. It was only when he reached the top step that he looked up, and for a moment he stood there gaping like a fish. His lips moved but at first no sound was formed. Then he managed to blurt out in a hoarse voice:

"Moshe the taxi driver, what are you doing here?"

To Ian's absolute astonishment, his erstwhile chauffeur of the previous day had somehow ended up behind the wheel of his hotel's shuttle bus, and was gazing down at him disdainfully from his perch at the wheel. (To this day Ian does not know how Moshe ended up there, but assumes that he was moonlighting to supplement his taxi-driver income.)

"Moshe, it's me, Ian. How are you, Moshe?"

The driver continued to gaze at him coldly.

"Moshe, it's me, your passenger from yesterday. You've got to forgive me!"

After a few more stony moments, Moshe's features softened slightly.

"*Sholom Aleichem,* Ian. Welcome aboard. And consider yesterday's incident forgiven and forgotten."

▪ Daughters and Sons

The Midrash describes how, while Rivkah was carrying her unborn twin sons, Yaakov and Esav, when she would pass by a synagogue or Torah study hall, the righteous child Yaakov would struggle within her, as if attempting to escape the womb. When she passed houses of idol worship, the evil child Esav would kick and squirm. This state of affairs greatly concerned Rivkah, and the verses describe how she went to consult with G-d, in an attempt to understand what indeed was transpiring with her pregnancy, and what would happen in the future. The verses then describe how Hashem answered her inquiries with an exact description of what would occur in the future, both to the boys themselves and to all their future offspring.

Our Sages tell us that she did not inquire directly of Hashem, but in fact traveled to the study hall of the great scholar Shem, also known as Malkitzedek, or "righteous king," who is described in the Torah as being a "Kohen to the One Above." It was Shem who informed her about her children's future, a prediction which was accurate down to the finest detail and one which still haunts us today. The Midrash learns from here that consulting a great Torah Sage is tantamount to inquiring of G-d Himself (Midrash Rabbah 63:6).

There is special Divine assistance which Hashem provides to Torah scholars, which ensures that no inaccuracies ever leave their mouths.

It is necessary to preface the next two stories with a perspective of my teacher Rav Aharon Pfeuffer, zt"l. His exact words were: "I do not like to tell stories like these, because these incidents do not define the greatness of a Torah giant like Rav Shmuel Rozovski, zt"l [the subject of both stories]. His greatness was [truly experienced] when one approached him to discuss a point in Torah study. His understanding! His knowledge! To sit in a shiur of Rav Shmuel Rozovski, just to see him delivering a shiur, was like seeing flames burning in dark clouds. As he spoke he paced from one side of the room to the other. It was fire. It is just impossible to describe the beauty of seeing him give a shiur. To see how after the shiur hundreds of young men tried to argue with him, keen young minds, and then watch him answer each one. A deep, deep mind. To see him in a shiur, I tell you, was more than all the miracles which can ever be." Nevertheless, these are the stories he subsequently told.

It was *Shabbos Shuvah* and Rav Pfeuffer was walking in the street when he met his Rebbe, Harav Shmuel Rozovski. The Pfeuffers were expecting a second child at the time, their first one having been a daughter; and after they greeted each other, the venerable teacher asked his student: "*Nu*, what are you hoping for?" Without much hesitation Rav Pfeuffer responded that he was hoping for another daughter. When questioned by Rav Rozovski as to why he was prejudiced toward the fairer gender, Rav Pfeuffer confessed that he was under the impression that daughters were easier to educate than their more rambunctious counterparts.

The *Rosh Yeshivah* replied to his student with the following words:

"No, you are a *Yekke* (a Jew of German descent), so if you had a daughter you will have a son, and then if you will have [another] daughter, you will have another son, and then you will have a daughter [and] you will have another son."

Rav Pfeuffer thought his teacher was humoring him.

The next day Yehudah was born.

... followed three years later by Naomi ...

... who was followed two years later by Menachem ...

... after which came Ruthi ...

... followed finally by Shlomo, some twenty years after the *Rosh Yeshivah's* apparently harmless quip.

In the words of Rav Pfeuffer: "I knew that whenever the *Rosh Yeshivah* said something, it never ever failed [to come true]. And that is what happened to us; it became so obvious."

Rav Pfeuffer related a second incident concerning his teacher, once again demonstrating the Rosh Yeshivah's *ability to make accurate predictions, even when what he said was apparently in jest.*

It was *Chol Hamo'ed* Pesach and a group of *bachurim* were sitting in the *beis midrash* savoring the fiery polemics of a page of Gemara — reading, refuting, suggesting, arguing, positing, toiling, enriching their minds and souls with the treasures of the Talmud and its commentators. The *Rosh Yeshivah* entered the room, and before long made a beeline to where Rav Pfeuffer was sitting. Peering over his young prodigy's shoulder, the *Rosh Yeshivah* became agitated at what he saw was being studied. "Tell me, R' Aharon," inquired the *Rosh Yeshivah*, "have you studied your *Halachah* today?" R' Rozovski regularly badgered R' Pfeuffer to study *Halachah*, an area often neglected by those who have experienced the exhilaration of learning Talmud.

Somewhat nonplussed by his Rebbi's patronizing manner, Rav Pfeuffer asked indignantly why out of more than twenty students in the room, the *Rosh Yeshivah* had singled him out on this count.

Hadn't all the students neglected their responsibilities toward the study of *Halachah* that day?

"Look, R' Aharon," the *Rosh Yeshivah* replied, "you like to travel. What will be if one day you end up in South Africa? There, it won't be enough for you to be sharp and fiery in Gemara. You will need to tell people what the practical *halachah* is when they come to ask you."

The students all began laughing at the wittiness of their *Rosh Yeshivah*. Travel into Africa at the time was the subject of jokes, somewhat akin to traveling to the moon or Mars. Who in their right mind would ever end up in such a far-flung and "G-d-forsaken" place?

Sure enough, within a few years Rav Pfeuffer was invited to travel to the South African city of Johannesburg, where he eventually found himself serving as the Rav of a thriving and vibrant community. It was there that he spent the last fourteen years of his life, disseminating Torah and, more specifically, ruling *Halachah* for the laymen of the community. It was from there that he published his classic halachic guidebooks on *kashrus* and family purity, and was able to ensure that South Africa would not be a G-d-forsaken place after all.

In concluding the story, Rav Pfeuffer described how, when he once traveled back to Eretz Yisrael, he stood reciting *Tehillim* by the grave of his late *Rosh Yeshivah*. Suddenly he was struck by a tremendous appreciation for his teacher, a man whose every word was so carefully chosen, uncannily accurate, and whose counsel was consequently so reliable.

▪ Timeless Advice

The following story requires the same perspective as the previous two, and is one which occupies a warm spot in my heart, for although some of its finer details have been consumed by the erosion of time, it is a story which transports me all the way back to my childhood, to the years I spent in close proximity to Rav Aharon Pfeuffer, z"tl. I could not have been much more than 10 years old at the time, yet I clearly recall the scene of the Rav sitting at the head of the seudah shelishis *table in the old yeshivah building, relating to his* talmidim *the wondrous event which had occurred to him on a trip to the Holy Land and the United Kingdom. The story he told went something like this.*

R av Pfeuffer maintained very close relationships with many of the great Torah Sages residing in Israel. He corresponded regularly with them and treasured every word he received in reply. He had a remarkable appreciation of the greatness of these leaders, and as a result, he succeeded in inculcating into two generations of his South African students a deep-seated awe and veneration of "the *gedolim.*" On his occasional visits to Eretz Yisrael, he would take the opportunity of seeking their counsel, and those of his students and congregants who were lucky enough to be in Israel at the time would often get the chance to tag along.

On this particular occasion, the Rav had entered the home of one of the great Sages residing in Bnei Brak. As he sat in the anteroom in expectation of his meeting, he noticed a young lady also seated in the room, who had just seen the *gadol.* Rav Pfeuffer noticed to his surprise that she was sobbing softly. After being warmly welcomed by the *gadol* and his wife, Rav Pfeuffer asked about the girl in the waiting room.

The Rebbetzin explained that the girl was engaged to be married. There is a custom in certain religious circles that the *kallah,* or bride-to-be, purchases for her future husband a gold watch which she presents to him after their engagement. This girl came from a destitute family, and did not have sufficient money to purchase the said piece of jewelry. Rav Pfeuffer was silent for a moment as he grasped the unfortunate situation. Then, without any further hesitation, he began removing his own solid gold watch from his wrist, which he handed to the Rebbetzin, asking her to pass it on to the girl.

The *gadol*, observing the magnanimous act taking place, turned to Rav Pfeuffer and praised him for his kindness. Then, as if as an afterthought, he added that Rav Pfeuffer need not worry about purchasing himself a new watch. Rav Pfeuffer was somewhat mystified by the Sage's statement, but chose not to pursue an explanation. The meeting continued as normal, and a short while later Rav Pfeuffer bade the Sage a warm farewell and left.

Although he had spent the majority of his years in Israel and South Africa, Rav Pfeuffer was in fact a descendant of a long line of German Jews. Members of the German Jewish community are known for their extreme punctiliousness, a characteristic which has at times made them the brunt of various jokes, the likes of which are normally used to conceal a genuine admiration by those less time-conscientious members of the faith. Thus it is safe to assume that it was a truly heroic act of self-sacrifice on the part of the Rabbi to surrender his timepiece.

What made the entire ordeal even more difficult to bear, however, was the advice of the Sage that Rav Pfeuffer not replace the watch, a piece of advice which was extremely difficult to observe, yet one which Rav Pfeuffer would not think of transgressing.

The Rabbi's itinerary included a short stay in London before his return to his hometown of Johannesburg. Thus, for the last few days of his visit to Israel, as well as for the duration of his stay in London, he gritted his teeth and tolerated the feeling of helplessness which came from being without a watch.

When the day of his flight to Johannesburg arrived he was suffering greatly without a watch, and was no doubt wondering what to make of the *gadol's* advice. He had to ask the time from various people throughout the day to ensure that he would not miss his flight, and he arrived at Heathrow International Airport without incident. After checking in his luggage and passing through passport control, the rabbi headed for the duty-free section of the waiting lounge with the intention of buying one or two things to take home.

As he stepped over the threshold of one of the large duty-free shops, there was a great commotion, and people started approaching him with big smiles on their faces. A man walked directly up to him, and shook the bewildered Rabbi's hand vigorously. "Congratulations, sir," exclaimed the man, obviously the manager of the store. "According to our door counter you are the one-millionth customer to walk through our doors! You are the proud winner of this gorgeous gold watch which we have reserved for this occasion.

"So once again, sir, congratulations!"

I vividly recall Rav Pfeuffer removing the watch to show us on that Shabbos afternoon after his return. To his thunderstruck students he emphasized the accuracy and reliability of *berachos* given by *gedolim*.

Indeed, he had received a timeless piece of advice.

▪ A Place to Call His Own

"… Anger is a very evil trait, and a person should avoid it at all costs. He should train himself not to become angry even for a good reason … The life of an angry man is not a life; therefore our Sages ruled that a man should distance himself from anger to the point that he can conduct himself without feeling even those things that evoke [justifiable] anger. This is the ideal path to follow and it is the way of righteous people, who suffer insults but do not insult, who listen to abuse that is leveled against them but do not respond, who do everything with love and who rejoice even when suffering pain …" (Kitzur Shulchan Aruch 29).

The following story illustrates the benefits of not angering easily. It also demonstrates a fascinating idea summed up in the words of the protagonist, Benny: "When you daven, you talk to Hashem, but when you learn, He talks to you."

There are few creatures in the world as territorial as the average shul-going Jewish male. His domain can consist of nothing more than a scrawny *shtender* tucked up against a battered chair in a corner of the synagogue, yet once he has declared the spot his own, he will often defend it to the very end. Now, although Benny Shein was only a migrant species passing through Jerusalem at the time of the following incident, the seat which he had found himself was in his mind one of the finest prayer locations in the world. The yeshivah in which the seat was found was located atop a gentle hill which overlooked the Jerusalem skyline, and the seat itself was situated alongside a giant window through which a refreshing breeze softly ruffled Benny's graying hair. One row ahead sat Benny's recently married son together with Benny's latest grandson, and immediately behind him sat a close family friend, Rabbi Pesach Mermelstein. Benny felt that the first Shabbos that he had spent in that seat was as close to Heaven as one could come. From the moment that the setting sun burnished the yellowing stones of the cityscape on Friday afternoon, until darkness settled over it on Saturday night, he felt an incredible sense of tranquility and happiness course through him.

The following Friday afternoon, Benny made sure to be at the yeshivah a few minutes early, to ensure that he could again occupy "his" seat. Once again the prayers and the sunset of the Friday-evening service combined into a fiery harmony, leaving Benny with a glow inside of him for the duration of the night. The following morning, Benny set out a little earlier than usual to reserve the seat, and once again he started his prayers there. It was only during the reading of the Torah that things did not go according to plan.

Benny was following carefully in his *Chumash* as the reader melodiously chanted the words of the weekly portion. Presently, they reached the section in the *parashah* of *Vayechi* where Yaakov calls together his twelve sons to stand alongside his deathbed, to speak with them for the last time before his death. Benny read with fascination that, while some of Yaakov's sons were given glowing praises and blessings, some of them were castigated for mistakes they had made in the past, and for ones that Yaakov predicted they would make in the future. About the firstborn son Reuven, he said, "[Because of] waterlike impetuosity – you cannot be foremost …"

Benny briefly scanned the commentary below and read how, as a result of the uncontrolled anger and impetuosity he had displayed at a certain point in his life, Reuven lost the rights to the birthright, the kingship, and the priesthood, the most coveted titles.

Suddenly, Benny sensed someone standing in front of him. Sure enough he looked up to see a tall, well-built young man looming over him. "That's my seat you're sitting in, sir," he said in a menacing and slightly sarcastic tone. Benny felt his blood boil as he realized that his favorite seat, his turf, was being challenged by this ill-mannered young man. He raised himself to his full height and prepared to do battle. In his mind he rehearsed his attack, certain that he would flatten the rude youngster into submission. ("Where were you last week, my friend?" he was about to shout. "And last night?" "You've missed most of today's service anyway!" "Don't you realize that I am a visitor and should be treated hospitably?")

But Benny held his tongue. It was clear to him that the youth had arrived at exactly this preordained moment, as Benny was reading in the weekly portion about the dangers of anger and impetuosity. There was no way he was going to get angry after experiencing such a freakish "coincidence." Without a moment's hesitation, Benny smiled at the young man, put his hand on his shoulder, apologized profusely, and vacated his favorite seat. The young man settled into the seat with a disdainful sigh and began to stare aimlessly out of the window.

For a moment Benny stood in the aisle feeling somewhat disoriented by his sudden eviction. Before he had a chance to claim another seat, he felt a tap on his elbow and turned to see the *Rosh Yeshivah* standing at his side with a warm smile on his face. The *Rosh Yeshivah* leaned closer and whispered in Benny's ear that he had witnessed the entire commotion over the seat. He told Benny that he was so impressed by his calm and peaceful reaction that he wanted Benny to sit alongside him in a position of honor at the front of the entire yeshivah. Benny gladly accepted the offer and was treated like a king for the duration of the service.

As Benny wended his way out of the yeshivah after the service, his friend Rabbi Pesach Mermelstein approached him. "You should know that it was an amazing thing that you did earlier on," he said. "Many people would have stood up and made a scene over that seat, for that kid was definitely out of line. What you must understand, however, is that this yeshivah is not for ordinary yeshivah students. The boys that come here are from broken homes, or from homes that have rejected them. Many of them have also been rejected by their friends, their communities, and even by society. In short, these boys have been completely rejected.

"What I wanted to tell you," said Rabbi Mermelstein, "is that many of these youngsters have nothing to treat as their own — nothing except their seat in the yeshivah. So, *yasher koach*."

▪ Prayer Flip

We live in a world of instant solutions: disposable crockery, fast food, and instantaneous communications to anywhere on the globe. We have come to expect these conveniences, at times even to demand them. It therefore comes as no surprise that people have become accustomed to running to great Torah leaders in the hope of finding painless, instant solutions to their problems.

There is no doubt that these people can help. Scholars who have immersed themselves in the Torah almost every waking moment of their lives have not only mastered its teachings, they have also gained the most incredible worldview, for in the Torah can be found the genes of the world: the reasons why the sea is blue, why the sun rises in the east, and the workings of the tiniest cell. There is no doubt that these sages are attuned to these matters and can be of great assistance to the troubled. Nevertheless we must remember that nothing in life that is valuable comes without effort. The following personal story was told to me by a very dear friend, and graphically illustrates the point.

Yaakov and Sara Maritzky moved to Israel shortly after their marriage, and settled in the vibrant new neighborhood of Ramat Beit Shemesh. It was a major adjustment for the two, who had both grown up in the relatively languid city of Johannesburg, but it was a challenge into which they threw themselves with much vigor and excitement. Yaakov enrolled in one of the numerous *kollelim* in the area, and Sara set about the task of turning their large apartment into a true Jewish home.

When they discovered that they were expecting their first child, much excitement filled their apartment in the Holy Land, as well as the homes of their respective parents thousands of miles away in Johannesburg. It was to be Yaakov's parents' first grandchild. After much negotiation, it was decided that the young couple would return to South Africa for the birth, in order to enable the grandparents to derive the necessary *nachas*, and to spoil the child as is the right of true Jewish grandparents. The tickets were booked, and Yaakov and Sara excitedly watched the days go by, as the time for their first child's arrival drew near.

In the eighth month of her pregnancy, on the day before they were due to fly to South Africa, Sara visited her doctor in Jerusalem for a regular checkup and ultrasound. All was in order, and according to the scan they were expecting a healthy child. However, the doctor regrettably informed her that due to the size of the baby and the fact that it was lying in the breech position, it was almost inevitable that she would have to deliver by cesarean section. Sara was greatly distressed by this news, as she would prefer to avoid a surgical procedure in favor of a natural delivery. She went home to discuss the news with Yaakov.

Sara's sister had suffered from similar complications during her pregnancies, and as Yaakov and Sara discussed their own situation, Sara recalled that her sister had received some unusual assistance with the problem. What she recalled was that her sister had consulted an elderly Rabbi in the heart of Jerusalem, who had prescribed a certain remedy, a remedy which had effectively turned her baby around into a more natural position. After some deliberation and a few phone calls, the Maritzkys resolved to see the Rabbi the following day.

The next morning, Yaakov and Sara were awake at 5 o'clock in the morning, and were waiting outside the apartment of the elderly and revered Sage at 8 o'clock sharp. Timing was of the essence: Their flight was departing later that night, and the Rabbi, who was old and frail, was only able to see a handful of visitors each day. When they finally entered the Rabbi's chamber, they described to him their predicament and waited expectantly for his response. The remedy which the man prescribed would have come as a great surprise to them, had they not been alerted beforehand by Sara's sister as to the nature of his recommendation. After thanking the elderly Sage profusely, they rushed out of the room to a waiting car and set out for the outskirts of Jerusalem.

They found the winding dirt road with little difficulty, and after some careful driving they came across the mountain stream gushing from the hillside as the Rabbi had described. They got out of the car and followed the stream up the slope toward its source. After walking for a few minutes they came to a small cavern, whence the stream originated. They entered the cavern gingerly. They found the exact spot the Sage had described, and carefully followed the instructions prescribed by the Rabbi, culminating in Sara drinking from the stream.

There was little time to savor the beautiful surroundings, and on completing the procedure, the young couple rushed back to the car. They had a flight to catch. The remainder of the day passed like a whirlwind, as they hurriedly packed their suitcases and raced to catch their plane. It was only when they finally sank into their seats on the airliner that they were able to digest the events of the day.

Two hours into the flight, Sara felt the baby moving.

A day after their arrival in South Africa, Sara visited a doctor, who confirmed what the couple already knew. The baby had turned over, and was lying in a completely natural position.

A few weeks later, Boruch Ber Maritzky was born to his over-joyed parents under completely natural conditions.

Postscript: A short time after the arrival of their child, Yaakov and Sara were told of another remarkable incident which occurred with the same Sage in Jerusalem, an incident which shed light on what exactly the power of his remedy is. A young couple was facing a similar predicament to the one that the Maritzkys had faced, namely that their baby was lying in a breech position. The couple had heard of the Rabbi's remedy, and instead of approaching the Sage directly, had bypassed him and headed straight to the mountain cave and the spring of water. They followed the procedure exactly as everyone else had, and then returned home. They waited and waited. Nothing happened.

After a few days the anxious couple arrived sheepishly at the Rabbi's door. They explained to him what they had done, and how it had not worked for them. The Rabbi looked them over sternly and berated them with the following remarkable words: "Do you think that I am a magician who hands out instant remedies? I pray for people! I personally *daven* for each and every couple that I send to that spring!" With that, he sent them back to the spring.

▪ Evil I?

Among the eight garments worn by the Kohen Gadol *(High Priest) was the* Choshen, *or Breastplate, a square, open-sided pocket, on the front of which was set twelve precious stones, each one inscribed with the name of one of the twelve tribes.*

Between the folds of the Breastplate was the Urim *and the* Tumim, *two scrolls upon which were written one of the ineffable Names of Hashem. The function of these two scripts was to assist the High Priest in making decisions of national importance. When he would contemplate the writing on the* Urim, *the various letters on the stones of the Breastplate would light up to spell out the answer to his question. This information, however, required interpretation, for the various letters could be arranged in a multitude of ways to spell out a diverse range of answers. This is where the* Tumim *came into play. The* Kohen Gadol *would then proceed to focus on the script on the* Tumim, *whereupon he would gain insight into the correct arrangement of the letters spelled out by the* Urim *(Ramban).*

Perhaps the workings of the Choshen *represent the way in which we receive messages from Hashem in this very day and age. Every person experiences Divine guidance at some stage in his life. Sometimes, however, a message is not so clear; the letters have lit up but we are not quite sure in which order to arrange them. It is at times like these that one must tread carefully, to seek the enlightenment such as the* Tumim *provided, either through painstaking, introverted soul-searching, or by consulting wise and experienced Torah leaders, to ensure that one correctly understands the message one has received.*

The following story is about someone who received a message, analyzed it, and would seem to have interpreted it correctly. Well, almost …

We were all sitting around the table after one of our regular Thursday-night *parashah shiurim*, trading stories and experiences. We were a motley group from a wide range of backgrounds; some of us had been religious all our lives, while others had trod a longer path to come to be sitting at that *shiur*, and the stories being told certainly bore this out. Suddenly, Shaun Simkin, who had been sitting and listening quietly at the end of the table, indicated that he had a story to tell. It is fascinating how a group of people can sense when a good story is about to be told – all the babble around the table quickly died down as all eyes turned toward Shaun.

"I don't often tell this story," he began, his eyes dropping for a second as he realized that he was now committed to continuing, "but it made a big impression on me, so I guess I will.

"I was in Israel, studying at a yeshivah known as Darchei Chaim, a small institution specializing in reintroducing wayward religious youths to the lifestyle which they had spurned during their teenage years. I was progressing nicely, and when an opportunity came to go tour the small northern town of Safed, I eagerly signed up. The word "Safed" always seemed to be associated with the word "mystical" in my mind, and conjured up images of holy men walking peacefully among timeless stone buildings, deep in meditation and thought. I was anxious to go and personally experience these images in real life.

"As I was leaving, one of the rabbis told me that in Safed there is a famous *mikveh*, a ritual bath known as the Arizal's *mikveh*, in which that famous kabbalist that was said to have regularly immersed himself. This rabbi told me that by immersing oneself in that *mikveh*, one is able to purify himself from sin and reach a high level of spiritual purity. He explained to me exactly how to go about the immersion.

"On my arrival in Safed, I immediately inquired as to the *mikveh*'s location, and was directed to the hallowed site. There, I set about readying myself for the immersion as the rabbi had instructed me. I untied my hair which was quite long at the time, and then set about removing my earring as I had been told to do. Then I removed the chain I was wearing around my neck, on the end of which dangled a small silver hand, a charm which reportedly has the power to ward off the *ayin hara* or evil eye. As I removed the necklace I was struck by a sudden pang of guilt, for I remembered that the trinket was not mine. I had pilfered it from a friend many years before. The feeling of guilt quickly passed as I once again focused on the matter at hand.

"I left my clothes and other possessions in a pile and entered the freezing water. There was no one else in the room so I was not concerned for the safety of my things. I proceeded to immerse myself as I was taught to do. Throughout the entire process not a soul entered the room.

"When I had completed my immersion, I climbed out of the *mikveh* and began dressing. As I reached for my shirt, my heart stopped for a moment. The "evil eye" was gone! I had left it lying next to the shirt together with my watch, which was still lying exactly where I had left it. I searched the area frantically, but the trinket was nowhere to be found. After many futile minutes of searching, I gave up on ever finding the charm, and left the *mikveh* feeling a lot less inspired than I had hoped to feel.

"As I walked through the narrow alleyways of that holy city, it suddenly dawned on me that maybe Hashem was trying to tell me something. Perhaps the charm got lost because I had stolen it in the first place? After a bit of serious thought I concluded that indeed this was the message, and since that day I have been exceedingly careful never to touch the possessions of others.

"I had gone into the *mikveh* to be purified from my sins, and indeed I was."

We were all duly impressed by Shaun's story, but someone immediately pointed out to him that there was one part of the incident which he may have misinterpreted. Although he no longer had the charm in his possession, there is no doubt that he still owed his friend the value of the stolen item.

Whether the trinket had simply fallen into a crevice which Shaun had overlooked, or whether it had been swallowed into a Divinely created cosmic black hole designed especially for such occasions, it is clear that Shaun was being sent a message. Nevertheless, the intention of the sign was, "That does not belong to you," as opposed to "You are now absolved from your crime." We must be extremely wary of misinterpreting our messages.

▪ Mitzvah Messenger

When our patriarch Yaakov sent his beloved son Yosef on his fateful mission to search for his brothers, a mission which was the precursor to his sale into slavery and the eventual exile of the entire Jewish people to Egypt, Yaakov told him, "Go, I will send you to them." This statement seems redundant; and the second part appears to have been added as an afterthought.

The reason for this was that immediately after instructing Yosef to "go," Yaakov became concerned about his favorite son's safety, for it was common knowledge that the brothers intensely despised their younger sibling. To reassure him that no harm would befall him on this mission, Yaakov told Yosef, "I will send you," thereby conveying mitzvah status upon the journey, the mitzvah of honoring one's father. Once it became a "mitzvah mission," Yaakov was certain that no harm could befall his precious son, for we have a principle that "one who is en route to perform a mitzvah will encounter no harm" (Kiddushin 39b).

Joseph indeed ended up in a harmful situation, including his near-death experience in the snake- and scorpion-filled pit, followed by his eventual sale into slavery by his brothers. The reason for this was that he was no longer covered by his father's mitzvah mission at that time. His father told him to go to Shechem. Yosef went there, heard that his brothers had departed, and then traveled beyond Shechem in search of them. Since he was no longer involved in a mitzvah, he lost his special protection and found himself in a dangerous situation (Ohr HaChaim).

On a recent trip to Israel, I was fortunate enough to experience firsthand the concept of a "mitzvah messenger" not meeting harm. This is what happened.

Graffiti never lies. I have always believed that the walls of a city tell its secrets, that graffiti is the muffled cry of a city's youth, an expression of the turmoil which roils inside the minds of local youngsters. In some cities, psychedelic colors emblazon the walls, reflecting the confusion and brain-numbing racket re-sounding in the heads of their young people.

The atmosphere in Israel was particularly tense. As I walked through the streets of a wintry Jerusalem, scrawls of black graffiti blurted out painful political rhetoric from the timeless golden stones of her walls, and I knew that difficult times lay ahead.

It was an awkward period to be visiting the Holy Land. Peace talks between the Israelis and the Palestinians were constantly wavering; on at breakfast time, off at lunch, and back on again in time to go to bed. There were too many unanswerable questions. Politicians claimed to have the answers, taxi drivers insisted they had the answers, housewives heatedly shared their own answers over the telephone lines. The only people who honestly believed in their heart of hearts that there were indeed answers, however, were a few patients languishing in the psychiatric wards of the tiny country's hospitals.

Every day on the roads connecting Israel's towns and cities, innocent citizens were being stoned, shot at, and intimidated by hordes of incited youths. The world press howled in self-righteous disgust, slamming the activities of the beleaguered Israeli Defense Force as it attempted to fight a war in which only *it* was expected to stick to the rules. And in the back of everyone's mind, including my own, was one great fear —

I heard the dreaded word as I was heading out of the yeshivah I happened to be visiting in Jerusalem. Someone had turned up the volume of the radio, ostensibly to share the news with those in the building, and as I heard *the* word on the news broadcast, I felt my throat clench and a terribly familiar feeling rise up from my gut. "*Pigu'a*" — a bombing. That was all I heard, but it was enough to stop me in my tracks. I tiptoed to the door and listened carefully for further details. "Tel Aviv"... "Number 51 bus"... "many injuries"... "police still combing the scene for other possible explosive devices." The snippets I managed to hear through the door sent tremors of apprehension through my very being. Questions flooded my mind, the same questions which were probably flooding the minds of millions of Israelis at that very moment. Was there perhaps someone I knew on the bus? A friend? A relative? Did it really make a difference? Aren't all Jews relatives? To make matters worse, I was scheduled to travel to Bnei Brak, a city neighboring Tel Aviv, within the hour. The chance of a second blast weighed heavily on my mind as I headed toward the bus station.

This was how the bombing was described the following morning in the *Jerusalem Post* (December 29, 2000):

> The terror attack for which Tel Aviv has been preparing came yesterday afternoon, when a bomb exploded on a bus, wounding 14. At 12:40, an explosion occurred on a No. 51 Dan bus as it passed Beit Kardan by the intersection of Derech Petah Tikva and Derech Namir, said Yarkon Precinct Chief Lt. Cmdr. Uri Bar-Lev.
>
> Police and municipal officials, who have been on alert for terror attacks for the past few months, said that it was a miracle that so few were injured, attributing it to luck and the quick response of emergency staff. Police found a medium-sized partially exploded pipe bomb in a bag on the back of the bus, [a] police spokeswoman said.
>
> Tel Aviv Police Chief Cmdr. Yossi Sedbon explained that the bomb was made up of several pipe bombs and other explosives, not all of which went off.

I arrived in Bnei Brak without incident at about 11 o'clock that night, which happened to be the eighth night of Chanukah. The purpose of my visit there was primarily to meet with Rav Yitzchak Zilberstein, *shlita*, Rav of the Ramat Elchanan neighborhood, world-renowned *posek*, and someone who has always greatly inspired me. I was scheduled to head back to Jerusalem the next day immediately after my early-morning appointment.

At 8 o'clock on Friday morning I found myself sitting in the waiting room nervously anticipating my meeting with the great leader. An assorted group of people also occupied the room. An elderly man sat apart from the others in one corner, deeply immersed in the problems he had obviously come to share with the Rabbi; a famous cartoonist engaged my companion in light conversation, while a few others whispered quietly among themselves. Soon a man slipped out of the Rabbi's consulting room and scurried through the waiting room without giving so much as a glance at the people seated there. A few eyes followed his hasty exit, but none of those present, myself included, paid much attention to his departure. A moment later, the door to the Rabbi's study opened again, and a second man exited. He paused in the waiting room, eyeing the handful of people gathered there. After a few moments of silence, he greeted a few of us, and then, glancing at the door through which his companion had disappeared, asked in a conspiratorial voice, "Do you know who he is?"

I looked at the others in the room. Everyone seemed to be as unfamiliar with the man in question as I was. Shaking our heads, we turned back to the speaker expectantly.

"That man," he informed us, "is my uncle."

He glanced toward the door as if to make sure that it was indeed closed, and then he dropped the bombshell.

"He was on *the* bus yesterday."

A hushed silence fell over the room, for everyone knew which bus he was refering to. The man in the corner surfaced from his reverie and leaned forward to hear the man more clearly.

This is the remarkable story he told:

"My uncle was at the vegetable market yesterday morning. He is in charge of ensuring the *kashrus* of the vegetables for the army, and often goes to the market to separate *terumah* and *ma'aser* from the army's purchases. After concluding his business there, he boarded the 51 bus headed in the direction of Beilinson hospital. As the bus traveled away from the *shuk*, he noticed a suspicious-looking man alight from the bus. At the following stop, some fifteen passengers disembarked, a detail which contributed to the low number of casualties, for it was immediately after that stop that the explosion occurred."

We were all mesmerized, as we tried to read the words off his lips faster than he could say them.

"The blast ripped through the bus, and for a moment after the deafening thunderclap, there was silence. Then people began to scream. Almost immediately, passersby began helping people off the bus. The scene was a grisly one, as victims stumbled out, bleeding profusely, their clothes in tatters."

He paused to compose himself before dropping his own bombshell:

"A woman seated two rows behind my uncle was critically injured. She sustained burns to 40 percent of her body. The man in the seat *next to* him was severely injured too. *Oy*, it was terrible. But as for my uncle … an absolute miracle … only his beard was slightly singed!"

One could almost hear the jaws going slack in the silent waiting room. We had all seen the man with our own eyes. But the young man's story was not finished.

"My uncle is a special man. He was on his way to perform an important task, and was not going to be deterred by the evil intentions of a cowardly terrorist. Minutes after stepping off the smoldering bus, he hailed a taxi. When a cab finally stopped, he instructed the driver to proceed to Beilinson Hospital. My uncle had been on his way to do one of the most esteemed *mitzvos* in our holy Torah, and he wasn't going to give it up so easily … He had been on his way to do *Taharas HaMeis*, voluntary purification of a deceased's body. In the end, he was only a few minutes late."

The police spokesperson attributed the miraculously low number of fatalities to luck and the quick response of the emergency services. We like to call it *hashgachah pratis*.

▪ A Brief Note on the War in Angola

t was a time when most of colonial Africa was being buffeted by what has become known as "the winds of change." European leaders were finding it increasingly difficult to justify their colonial positions in Africa, while black Africans began rallying together to oust their white oppressors for the sake of "uhuru," freedom and self-determination.

For many years, Portuguese Angola seemed impervious to the change sweeping through this troubled continent. The right-wing dictatorship in Lisbon seemed indomitable; the three black rebel groups fighting for Angolan independence were being firmly kept in their place by large numbers of young Portuguese troops. Ironically, it was these very troops that eventually led to the transition that no one thought would ever happen. In 1974, a group of military officers, probably influenced by their bitter comrades serving time in far-off colonies, overthrew the government in Portugal and immediately began a major decolonization program. In January 1975, Angola was granted independence, to be governed ostensibly by representatives of the three rebel groups. Unfortunately, each group wanted to head the government on its own, and the resulting power struggle turned into a bloody civil war.

From across the globe, communist Russia, under the leadership of Leonid Brezhnev, saw new potential in this far-off African land. Marxist-Leninist governments had recently been installed in Poland, Hungary, and East Germany while further afield, similar governments were being established in Vietnam, Cambodia, and Laos to complement the long-established members such as Cuba. With remarkable alacrity, Moscow identified one of the three rebel groups, the Marxist MPLA (Popular Movement for the Liberation of Angola) as a suitable protégé for its budding social-imperial ambitions, and began backing the group with weapons, finances, and manpower.

The Western powers, reeling from their defeat in Vietnam, were less decisive in their reaction to the unfolding drama, but nevertheless began supporting the remaining two parties, UNITA (National Union for the Total Independence of Angola) and the short-lived FNLA (National Front for the Liberation of Angola) which later merged with UNITA. Between November 1974 and February 1976, Moscow sent an estimated $400 million worth of weaponry to Angola and backed the landing there, in support of the MPLA, of a Cuban military expeditionary force which by mid-1976 was some 11,000-strong. The United States response was to send its own allies, some $32 million in arms, the maximum that the C.I.A. was permitted to supply covertly under United States law. Angola had become the third world chessboard on which the Big Powers could compete ideologically and, through their representatives, even militarily.

In 1976, the MPLA defeated its enemies and formed a Marxist government. But the war was far from over. UNITA retreated into the bush, where it regrouped and began launching guerrilla attacks on government forces. It was at this stage that South Africa sneaked into the war, ostensibly to defend its borders from the threat of communist invasion. From its bases in northern Southwest Africa, the apartheid regime dispatched large brigades of armored vehicles and tanks as well as heavy artillery northwards deep into Angola to bolster the beleaguered UNITA. Airstrikes were also launched from these bases, although they were severely hindered by enemy air superiority. In the ensuing decade and a half, Cuba increased its presence to some 50,000 men. Russia contributed in excess of $5 billion in arms and supplies to the MPLA. In late 1988, South Africa and Cuba signed an agreement whereby South Africa committed itself to stop sending aid to UNITA, while the Cubans agreed to withdraw from Angola entirely.

During the course of South Africa's involvement in the war, numerous Jewish men were drafted into the armed forces and were sent to the front, where they experienced firsthand the atrocities of war. Many are to this day deeply affected by their experiences.

▪ Sharp Knife

*Our Sages explain that the name "Yisrael" is in fact a mnemonic, which stands for the expression "***Y***esh ***S***hishim ***R***ivuy ***O***siyos **L**a Torah." Directly translated, this means, "There are sixty myriad letters in the Torah," and it refers to the fact that the Torah is made up of a total of 600,000 letters. This connection, between the title of the Jewish people and the tally of the letters in the Torah, alludes to the fact that the total number of Jews at Sinai was 600,000. Hence every Jew represents one letter in the Torah, a tiny element, but one which when absent or damaged can invalidate the entire Torah. (See* Sefer HaToda'ah *Chap. 30 for a more extensive discussion of how these figures are calculated.)*

The following is a story of a Jewish neshamah, *one of those letters of our* sefer Torah, *that was saved thanks to a remarkable piece of Divine synchronicity. The story appears as told to me by its protagonist, and also demonstrates the advice of the Talmud:*

Ki afilu cherev chadah munachas al tzavaro shel adam al yimna atzmo min harachamim — *For even if a sharp knife rests on a person's neck, he should not withhold himself from [praying for] Divine mercy* (Berachos 10).

The intensive care ward of the Linksfield clinic is similar to facilities of its kind the world over. Nothing moves in the ward, save the occasional nurse scurrying across the room to adjust a monitor or change a drip. The only signs of life come from the methodical beep, hum, and whoosh of the myriad life-giving gadgets attached to about a dozen patients convalescing there. An ironic relationship exists between these machines and the patients hooked up to them. If the machine stops, the patient does too; if the patient stops, the machine joins him. After a few days in the draining environment of the ward, one actually begins to wonder who is supporting whom.

It was in this setting that Malcolm Chesno found himself in late November 1998, recovering from a major neck operation. The procedure had been a success and he had been moved to the ward earlier in the day. The night shift had relieved their exhausted daytime colleagues a few hours earlier and had bedded down the patients for the night. Suddenly, one of the machines above Malcolm's bed began beeping frantically. A nurse jumped up to investigate, expecting to find a problem with the monitor rather than with the patient it was monitoring. To her horror, she found Malcolm in respiratory distress and unable to speak. Her mind went blank as she tried to remember the correct procedure for such a crisis. Before she had a chance to respond, and without any warning, the door to the ward suddenly swung open and Malcolm's surgeon walked in! He had decided to pay an unscheduled late-night visit to the ward, and had arrived just in time to save his patient's life. He was to be the first of three unexpected guests during the long night that followed.

The cause of the distress seemed to be related to the surgery he had had earlier. A hematoma had formed in Malcolm's neck and was obstructing his airway, making breathing almost impossible. After some hasty deliberation, the surgeon decided to have Malcolm rushed back into the operating room for emergency surgery to relieve the blockage. As two nurses were speedily pushing the bed down the corridor toward the surgical ward, one of the bed's corners bumped against the wall. A passerby, noticing the need for more hands, grabbed the corner, and joined the procession rushing through the hallways. This passerby was Rabbi Menachem Raff, and as he sped along next to the bed, he glanced down at its occupant. His heart nearly ground to a complete halt as he recognized the face, which was by now contorted in pain. Malcolm had been a regular in Rabbi Raff's shul and had become quite close to the Rabbi! Surprise guest number two had arrived.

As the surgery got underway it became apparent that it was going to be no simple exercise to save Malcolm's life. The anesthesiologist was unable to obtain an airway and the surgery commenced without an anesthetic! While the surgeon delicately worked his way toward the problem area, the anesthesiologist dashed out of the operating room, hoping to find a more experienced colleague to assist with the troublesome airway.

Many years earlier, Malcolm had served time in the South African Defense Force on the border with Angola. His position was that of a medic but because he is a talented cook, his culinary flair had earned him the ad hoc position of kosher chef for the Jewish combatants in the forward base of Ondangwa. One of his patrons happened to be Dr. Milton Blackman who was serving as a field doctor in the camp. The men became close friends, a relationship which helped both of them survive the fierce and bloody war being fought between the South Africans and the Marxist Angolan forces. After the war, Malcolm and Milton went their separate ways but the two remained good friends. During the war years, Malcolm had seen Milton save countless lives and he often joked that if he was ever in need of resuscitation, Milton was the man he wanted for the job.

It was Dr. Milton Blackman who was the third surprise guest of the evening. He had been visiting a patient in one of the other wards, when Malcolm's panic-stricken anesthesiologist came bursting through the doors looking for assistance. Milton by that stage had numerous years of experience in anesthesiology under his own belt, and hurried out after his colleague to lend a hand. Within minutes, Dr. Blackman established an airway and the hematoma was released.

Malcolm's life had been saved thanks to the coolheadedness of his surgeon, the experience of his old friend the anesthesiologist, and the reassuring manner of his rabbi. All three "just happened" to be present that night.

▪ Elephant

In the very first of the Rambam's thirteen principles of faith, Ani Ma'amin, we say as follows:

"I believe with a complete faith that the Creator, Blessed is His Name, creates and guides all creatures, and that He alone made, makes, and will make everything."

This creed sums up the concept of Hashgachah P'ratis, the fundamental principle which is probably best translated in simple terms as "personal attention," meaning that Hashem is aware of the minutest details in the world, and responds and reacts in accordance with the actions of every person. We are obliged to open our eyes to the fact that no occurrences are random or a result of luck of the draw, and that every moment of our existence is completely dependent on His attention. The following story was described to us by Rabbi Eliezer Sandler — who today lives in the United States — on a recent visit of his to South Africa.

The tiny camouflaged plane skimmed along the treetops somewhere over the scorching grasslands of Southern Angola. This unusual altitude was maintained throughout the flight, not by choice but rather out of necessity. The enemy possessed sophisticated antiaircraft missiles, designed to chase down and destroy high-speed fighter jets. Obliterating the tiny propeller-driven plane with one of these weapons would be childishly simple. The small plane banked sharply and touched down on a rugged bush strip, taxied, and came to a halt alongside a large green tent. The door opened and a bearded figure stepped out: Rabbi Sandler has arrived. A well-built man with a large skullcap, his upright bearing communicated an air of importance. The year was 1976.

For the chief chaplain of the South African Defense Force (SADF), this type of trip was routine. Among his numerous other responsibilities, it was his duty to visit all the various battle camps along the border during the war, ensuring that the Jewish fighters' special needs were being met. Not only did he supervise their spiritual well-being, but he made it his business to monitor their physical health too. The small single-engine plane was reserved for his own use.

By and large the SADF was good to the Jews fighting for the South African cause in Angola. Kosher food was always readily available, funds were provided to purchase *Chumashim, siddurim,* and other vital religious material. Once a year a ceremony was even held during which the chief chaplain would "rent" for a one-year period all the army bases in the entire theater of operations from the Defense Force. This was done so that they would be considered private Jewish property, thereby making it permissible for the Jews to carry within the enclosed common areas on Shabbos. (Rabbi Sandler relates how the officer in charge took this transaction so seriously that he made sure to mention each year that although the property belonged to the chaplain, he was not permitted to build on it!)

Over the years Rabbi Sandler has encountered some fascinating stories on his hops from camp to camp counseling the battle-weary young men. On this occasion, the chief chaplain had "dropped in" to check on three Jewish soldiers recuperating in the sick bay of a tiny advance base near the border.

He approached the medic tent quietly, not certain what lay behind the gently fluttering walls of canvas. Surreptitiously, he craned his neck around the doorway before announcing his presence, as was his custom on such visits. A large amount of information can be gleaned simply by observing the outward appearance of an ailing man, and this information can sometimes prove extremely valuable to a visiting rabbi. Through the gloom of the tent, he slowly made out the prostrated forms of the three men, each contemplating the expanse of green canvas above his own stretcher as if all three had simultaneously discovered it to be a source of tremendous fascination. The first soldier appeared to have broken his leg; a long white cast rose up from his hip and was suspended from a hook on the ceiling connected to his toe by means of a shiny silver chain. It appeared as if someone had run out of inspiration halfway through the process of mummifying him. The second man was clearly recuperating from a bout of some disease — probably malaria or dysentery, the Rabbi's experience told him, as indicated by the unusual pallor of his countenance. It was the third man that baffled him. There were no casts or plaster of paris to give clues to the state of the man's orthopedics, nor any discoloration of the visage to indicate any form of illness. Strangely enough, the man appeared to be a remarkably healthy specimen, far too healthy, in fact, to be languishing in a hospital cot.

Satisfied that he had gleaned all he could from his clandestine observations, the Rabbi entered the tent and introduced himself to his three co-religionists. Turning to the first, he inquired as to how the man had succeeded in fracturing his leg. The man proceeded to describe the clash that had almost claimed his life, in the end only costing him six weeks of mobility.

After a few minutes of counseling, he wished the man a *refuah sheleimah* and then turned to the second warrior. "And when," he asked gravely, "did you pick up this malaria?" The patient was mildly surprised by the Rabbi's rapid diagnosis, and he proceeded to describe to him what he had endured.

The chaplain turned to study the third man. The more he studied him, however, the more he was certain that the man should have been out on the battlefront, rather than lying flat on his back contemplating the roof of a hospital tent. After a few moments he conceded defeat. "I give up, my boy. Tell me, what are *you* doing here?"

"Well actually, Rabbi," the man drawled slowly, evidently enjoying the suspense and attention, "actually — I was stood on by an elephant."

A look of glee crossed his countenance as he watched the Rabbi's look of surprise. And indeed, Rabbi Sandler had been rendered speechless, not a common occurrence for any rabbi. When he managed to regain his breath and begged for further details, this was the remarkable narrative which unfolded:

"My name is Lance and I am a special forces' operative, attached to a reconnaissance battalion. As you may know, our job in this war is to spend time behind enemy lines, causing them as much grief as possible, while at the same time gleaning important intelligence for headquarters. Last week we were once again dropped behind the lines by a chopper; there were six of us on the team. Our orders were to try and monitor the movements of the enemy and report back to headquarters if they made any unscheduled maneuvers. On the team we each have a role; on this particular excursion I was acting as the radio operator and had to carry the large radio pack on my back."

Rabbi Sandler listened with fascination as the man continued:

"On the second day, we were moving through the brush quietly, when the group leader raised his hand, a silent order to halt. Up ahead we heard the sounds of bushes being broken and we all immediately readied ourselves for a clash with the enemy. The next signal from the leader had us puzzled for a while, for he had placed his elbow on his nose and with a grin began waving his arm around comically. We eventually did figure it out, but not before he placed his finger on his lips and indicated to us to advance slowly and quietly. As you probably know, we "recces" may be tough fighters, but we also know how to have a bit of fun. What is there to be scared of when you're in enemy territory anyway and are armed to the hilt? Here was the perfect opportunity for some fun.

"The elephant was standing in a clearing eating the topmost branches of a small tree he had just knocked over. Fortunately we were downwind from him and he was unaware of our presence. Suddenly, without warning, one of our men bolted into the clearing and charged straight at the large gray beast, howling ferociously. It was a very brave move and one which he was certain would gain him respect among his mates back in the mess tent. Two tons of elephant nearly jumped out of its baggy gray skin as the poor creature reeled from the shock. Nevertheless, the creature recovered quickly and with a loud trumpet blast charged after its fleeing attacker, who in turn ran back toward us.

"Not one of us managed to get a single shot off before we were forced to turn and run for our lives. Most of the guys dropped their weapons at the sight of the massive creature bearing down on them. An instant later, the adrenaline kicked in and we ran like men possessed. To my abject horror, I found myself lagging behind, weighed down by the heavy radio pack. A root protruding from the ground made me trip and suddenly I found myself lying face down in the soft sand, with two tons of pachydermal fury bearing down on me."

Silence filled the tent. The other men had probably heard the story numerous times but they were fascinated by the look of the spellbound Rabbi.

"What happened next is all pretty much a blur in my memory. There was very little sound and then suddenly— woomf! I felt tremendous pressure on my back and then I heard the sound of the radio crushing. A giant shadow raced over me and then went thundering into the bushes. I lay there, listening to the sounds receding into the bush and wondered if I was still alive. A shout came from a nearby bush. "Lance, you okay?" followed by another similar call from a second bush, then a third, a fourth, and a fifth. I didn't really know whether I was okay so I just grunted in reply. I felt them lifting me out of the indentation in the sand and the next thing I knew I was standing on my feet. An impromptu examination revealed no major damage, except for one or two painful bruises and a couple of minor lacerations. Now they've got me here under observation. Um — that's basically my story."

On his way out of the camp, a flabbergasted Rabbi Sandler was shown the radio which had saved Lance's life. A standard mobile radio transmitter at the time was approximately twelve inches thick. This one had been squashed to almost half its original thickness!

Despite Rabbi Sandler's efforts to spiritually arouse Lance after the incident, he never heard from him again, and often wonders whether the young man even took note of the miracle that had been performed for him.

▪ Legacies

The Tabernacle which traveled with the Israelites in the desert was assembled by Bezalel the son of Uri, a man blessed with a prodigious general knowledge coupled with an insightfulness that allowed him to understand and integrate the many subjects that he came across. Added to this, he was granted great talent as a craftsman, not to mention Ruach HaKodesh, *or spiritual intuition, to which he was privy.*

The Torah generally designates people by their first names, or occasionally by adding the name of their father for greater clarity. It is interesting to note the unusual way in which the Torah refers to Bezalel, constantly mentioning his grandfather Chur.

This could be to hint to us the reason why Bezalel merited the talents needed to build the Mishkan. *When the Jewish nation disgraced themselves by constructing the Golden Calf, it was Chur's objection that was heard the loudest. Chur was a man not afraid to stand up for his convictions even at great risk to his life, and he refused to have anything to do with the Calf. When the people saw that Chur would not assist them, he was brutally killed.*

Chur was martyred while trying to prevent the massive desecration of Hashem's Name which would result from the Golden Calf.

Thus, when the time came to construct the Mishkan, *which was to be the* mashkon, collateral, *for the sin of the Golden Calf, it was Bezalel the grandson of Chur who merited to bring it to reality. The grandfather gave his life in a futile attempt to prevent the damage; the grandson merited to be the one to repair it* (Kli Yakar).

The legacy of a good deed is eternal, and will remain in the world as a merit for many later generations.

This was experienced firsthand by a close family friend, who told me the following story.

M alcolm Schwartz was fortunate in his misfortune. Pretoria was being sucked deeper and deeper into the conflict in Angola at the time, and as a doctor, he had no chance of avoiding conscription into the South African Defence Force, or SADF. Doctors had become invaluable to the bloody, casualty-ridden conflict. Malcolm, however, was fortunate that the post of chaplain was vacant at the time in a camp called Grootfontein, a base in Southwest Africa some 250 kilometers south of the battlefront. This position ensured that he was safe from any real action at the front.

The SADF of the 1970's worked on a two-tier ranking system. Non-commissioned officers or NCOs bore their rank on their arm and were primarily drawn from less-educated sectors of the population. Commissioned officers were usually more qualified than their noncommissioned counterparts, often bearing an academic degree of some form, and wore their rank on their shoulder. Commissioned Officers were senior in rank to noncommissioned officers, such that the most decorated NCO would still have to salute the most low-ranking CO. As a doctor, Malcolm was ranked as a commissioned officer.

Malcolm must have been an interesting sight, dressed in his regulation blue medic's uniform, yarmulka perched on his head and very unmilitary beard jutting from his chin declaring his chaplaincy. It was this sight that probably captured the interest of Regiment Sergeant Major Mathews and the overall commander of Grootfontein, as he passed the medics tent one day. Malcolm was standing outside the tent talking with a Lebanese colleague by the name of Kuri. "I see the Arabs and the Jews are getting along nicely," quipped Mathews as he passed, quite tickled by his own drollness. As a commissioned officer, Malcolm was not obligated to salute the RSM, an NCO, and hence he was not overly intimidated by him, despite his overall stature in the camp. He was surprised at the remark, however, and braced himself for some unpleasantness. Fortunately the RSM kept walking, and the confrontation dissipated.

A few days later, Malcolm once again found himself outside the medic's tent, easing his mind from the tension and strain of piecing together young men, shot to bits fighting a seemingly futile war. Once again Mathews walked past, but this time he stopped. "So how are the Jews doing, chaplain?" he asked, his voice indicating neither sarcasm nor sincerity. Malcolm readied himself for the confrontation he was expecting.

"The Jews are well, sir," he replied guardedly.

"And the food," continued the RSM. "What is the situation with the kosher food?"

Grootfontein also happened to house the central SADF kosher kitchen; hence it was one of Malcolm's many duties to ensure that sufficient kosher food was always available for the Jewish fighting men.

"The kosher food is plentiful and delicious," Malcolm replied; the former adjective was an exaggeration while the latter was an outright lie.

"And on the battle front," the RSM interrogated. "What about Oshakati and Ondongwa?"

"Plenty in both, sir."

"I am glad to hear that," said the RSM, "and if you need any help, feel free to approach me."

The chaplain was flabbergasted. What on earth could the sergeant major be talking about? By the way Mathews stood there, with a faraway look in his eyes, it was clear to Malcolm that he had a story to tell, although what the story could possibly be eluded him completely.

Malcolm's quizzical looks prompted Mathews to explain his unusual offer:

"I grew up in Johannesburg, in a neighborhood known as Doornfontein. As you probably know, Doornfontein was the cradle of Johannesburg Jewry, the refuge for thousands of Jews fleeing the turmoil of pre-World War Europe. Despite the fact that our family was not Jewish, we settled among the Jews, patronizing their stores and befriending them. I even attended a Jewish *cheder*.

"When World War II broke out, my father was drafted into the army and was sent up north to fight the Germans, leaving my mother alone to support the family. Times were tough and our family began to founder. Money was so scarce that we could barely afford the groceries we normally purchased at the local Jewish grocery store.

"One day, my mother entered the store, chose a few items, and proceeded to the counter to pay for her meager purchases. At the counter, Mr. Rubinstein, the proprietor of the store, contemplated my mother's choices for a few moments. Old Mr. Rubinstein understood the situation. With a firm voice, he instructed her to take the purchases home without paying. 'Payment can wait until your husband returns,' he offered graciously. 'I know what it's like not to have a breadwinner around.' Moved by his perceptiveness, my mother accepted the benevolent gesture, more out of necessity than anything else."

Malcolm's heart began to swell as he listened to the benevolence of his people, being described by this gentile, deep in the African bush.

"After the war, my father returned home to his family. On hearing of our thoughtful benefactor, he immediately hurried to the store, war pay in hand, to remunerate Mr. Rubinstein. After thanking the grocer effusively for supporting our family so graciously, my father took out his money to pay the outstanding debt. Without a moment's hesitation, Mr. Rubinstein pushed my father's proffering hand away. 'Don't even think of it, Mr.

Mathews,' he announced firmly. 'You have just arrived home from the war. Take this money and spend it on your wife and kids. My debt can wait a while.'

"Ever since I arrived in Angola," continued Regiment Sergeant Major Mathews, "I have made it my business to ensure that the Jews always have sufficient food. At times there were shortages of kosher rations for the Jewish soldiers at the front in Oshakati and Ondongwa. I personally drove up there in my van to deliver the necessary supplies."

"I do it for old Mr. Rubinstein," explained the sergeant major.

▪ House on Fire

Atraveler once passed through a large city. On reaching its outskirts, he was horrified to see a beautiful but empty house with huge flames bursting from its windows and a pillar of smoke gushing from its uppermost extremities. With rising panic, the man desperately scanned the area in the hope of spotting an owner, someone intent on rescuing the building, or someone to at least grieve over its destruction. It cannot be, thought the traveler, that such a beautiful edifice could be without an owner or maker.

In much the same way as it was obvious to the traveler that the building had to have a creator, so too it should be obvious to us that the perfect and beautiful world that we live in cannot be without a Maker. All too often, we walk past the "building," not stopping for a moment to contemplate the fundamental and existential question of its origin. Unfortunately, it often takes a dramatic and at times traumatic conflagration to draw our attention to this reality.

Throughout this collection, I have documented many events which seem to center around disaster: crime, natural catastrophes, road accidents, and the like. It seems that, unfortunately, it takes events like these to make us realize that, indeed, this "building" has a Maker.

The following story encapsulates this idea, and with it I conclude this collection.

"There's a house on fire!" The cry from one of my students only penetrated the very edge of my consciousness. I was engrossed in my Gemara, urgently reviewing the day's material one last time before the start of the morning classes, and was not eager to be disturbed. I considered ignoring the exclamation, but something in his voice told me that this time it was not a prank. I dashed outside and followed the gazes of a small throng of students gathered on the school lawn. Sure enough, tufts of gray smoke curled out of the windows of a house not two hundred meters away, then crept up the slant of its roof and came together in a great black pall climbing skywards.

"The fire brigade!" someone suggested in a panic-stricken voice. "Already been called," came the reply. I stood rooted to the spot. A group of men raced toward the house, perhaps in the hope of helping the occupants, perhaps only to quell the rising feeling of helplessness. I gaped in morbid fascination, unable to move, as large flames began licking the outside walls to the sounds of exploding glass. A siren was heard; help had arrived. The bustle of firemen, daunted by the drama, amid a tangle of red hoses. The hiss of water quenching the flames' insatiable thirst. The gray pillar turned white as smoke was replaced by steam. The fire died.

A distraught man stood alongside the smoldering shell, which yesterday was his home. As the firemen scratched around inside, extinguishing the last few embers, the man told a chilling story. This had been his home that he shared with his wife and infant child. "This time of morning," he stammered, peering involuntarily at his watch, "they are normally fast asleep." His gaze slowly took in the scene of devastation. "Yesterday, a friend just happened to ask if we would look after their house for them while they went away." He paused —

"We didn't sleep here last night."